GORDON SETTERS TODAY

José Baddeley

New York

Maxwell Macmillan Canada
Toronto

Maxwell Macmillan International
New York   Oxford   Singapore   Sydney

HOWELL BOOK HOUSE
A Prentice Macmillan Company
15 Columbus Circle
New York, NY 10023

Library of Congress Cataloging-in-Publication data

Baddeley, José.
  Gordon Setters today / by José Baddeley.
      p.   cm.
   ISBN 0-87605-183-2
   1. Gordon setters.   I. Title
  SF429.G67B34 1994 94-5026 CIP
  636.7'52 – dc20

Manufactured in Singapore
10 9 8 7 6 5 4 3 2 1

ACKNOWLEDGEMENTS

I am indebted to the following for their assistance in putting this book together: Bert and Mary Dyde, who have done most of the photography, also Peter Howard and Graeme Murray. Jenny Simpson for research into Fochabers.
And to all those lovely people who own Gordon Setters everywhere, for their kind co-operation in supplying photographs and historical data from all over the world.

I dedicate this book to my daughter Deborah because, indirectly, she is almost as responsible for its contents as I am. Over the years she has encouraged my involvement with dogs and without the time she gave up I could not have continued. Deborah has been dog sitter, cleaning lady, midwife, mentor, hostess and general cook and bottle washer. It is to her that I say many times over...Thank you.

Jose Baddeley and her Lourdace Gordon Setters.

Bert and Mary Dyde.

INTRODUCTION

From early childhood I have lived with animals of all kinds. I find them fascinating and they give me no trouble at all. Yet since my involvement with Gordon Setters and the work that I have done with 'Rescue', I have become increasingly aware that a lot of people do suffer problems, especially with dogs. This is seldom the dog's fault but is caused by the ignorance of the owners.

As there has been no publication devoted specifically to Gordons, this book will, hopefully, fill that gap and be a help to all owners, or prospective owners, of this lovely breed.

I have written it in layman's terms, to make for easier understanding both of my own experiences and those of others. I would like every owner of a Gordon to receive as much pleasure from their dogs as I have had from mine.

The world is a richer place when you are able to build a rapport with your dog. And please remember: No dog is ever born bad – any problems which develop are the result of human failure.

I trust this book will help you to have many happy years with the Gordon Setter of your choice.

6

Chapter One

ORIGINS OF THE BREED

THE BEGINNINGS OF THE GORDON
The Gordon Setter is one of two Gundog breeds that are natives of Scotland. Although credit for the existence of the Gordon is given to Alexander, the 4th Duke of Gordon (1743-1827), there are many different stories as to how the breed was really established. The best-known one is that the Duke, realising that his shepherd had a black and white collie bitch who was good at game-finding, mated her to his current setters, and this resulted in the early Black and White Setters. If this was so, then it would have been an isolated outcross, and have little bearing on any future litters. The idea that this is how the breed actually originated has not been proved and is likely to be nothing more than hearsay, as there were Black and Tan

Alexander, Duke Of Gordon (1743-1827) is credited for the existence of the Gordon Setter.

Gordon Castle at Fochabers: the seat of the Dukes of Gordon.

setters in existence as early as 1600. The seat of the Dukes of Gordon was at Gordon Castle, which is sited near to the mouth of the river Spey, close to Fochabers. Sadly, it is, today, only a ruin, due to a fire at some time in the mid 1980s, but it is still an object of interest to many avid 'Gordoners' from overseas, who take in the journey to visit it as part of a holiday and in the hope of securing a good photograph to add to their Gordon memorabilia. While it is not exactly clear when the 4th Duke began his famous strain of 'Castle' Setters, it is documented that there were black and fallow setters in Elizabethan times, though this has been disputed as being based on many misquotations from a prolific early 17th century writer.

THE EARLY USE OF SETTERS

The setter was certainly evolved from a spaniel, and setting spaniels, originally imported from Spain, were in use by the 16th century. Taking time to consider the way of life of those times gives an insight into the workings of an estate and the importance of the dogs which were kept. The hunting of birds was mainly for food for the table, especially on the estuaries and river mouths where large flocks of geese, among others, would be readily available. Hawking was the first means of catching birds. A dog was needed to set, or crouch, and indicate the position of sitting game. Then, on command, the dog would flush the bird and the hawk would be released to catch it. Netting was the other method used, which required the dog not only to acknowledge game by pointing, but to crouch so low that gamekeepers could draw a net over the dog in order to catch the quarry. This method would do the least damage to the birds, so the keepers could extract the younger ones and release them, to enable breeding to continue.

During this period of history, dogs were often given as presents to other dignitaries and also to the rulers of other countries. This led to the breeding of one strain of setter to another and, while the original colouring of the Gordon Castle Setters was predominantly black and tan, many had white markings as well. The 4th Duke is known to have used setter stud dogs from the Earl of Leicester's kennel and, possibly, setters from other sources. Both the Duke and the Earl are recorded as having black, white and tan dogs and it is written that they preferred the tricolour, as it showed up better on the moors. This may well have brought about an increase in the number of dogs of this colour. However the primary consideration of both kennels was to produce excellent workers.

CHANGES IN GORDON KENNELS

Alexander the 4th Duke, died in 1827. His estate was inherited by George, the 5th Duke, who sadly died in 1836, having only owned Gordon Castle for some nine years. There is no doubt that, during these years, the kennel was considerably reduced in number. It is probable that many of the setters were given away to friends and, possibly, to the Duke's gamekeepers. At any rate, in July 1836, at one of Tattersall's famous auctions, only eleven Gordons were offered for sale. As these were probably the residue of the kennels, it gives a hint of what this establishment had contained at the height of its glory.

Here is a fascinating list of the dogs, their new owners and the prices paid for them.

1. Duke. 5 years, a black and tan dog, by his Grace's famous Old Regent ex Ellen. 34 guineas to Lord Abercorn.
2. Young Regent. 4 years, a black and white and tan, by Old Regent ex Ellen. 72 guineas to Lord Chesterfield.
3. Juno. 5 years, black and white, by Old Regent ex Juno. 34 guineas to Duke of Richmond.
4. Satan. 2 1/2 years, black dog, by Blunder ex Juno. 56 guineas to Lord Douglas.
5. Crop. 3 years, black and white bitch, by Lord Sultoun's Range ex Bell. 60 guineas to Lord Chesterfield.
6. Duchess. 11 months, black and white bitch, by Dash ex Crop, pupped August 20th 1835, was hunted this spring but not shot to. 37 guineas to Mr Martyn.
7. Random. 10 months, red and white dog, by Ranger ex Romp, pupped September 10th 1835, was hunted this spring but not shot to. 35 guineas to Mr Martyn.
8. Princess. 11 months black and white bitch, by Dash ex Crop, pupped August 20th 1835, not broken. 25 guineas to Mr Walker.
9. Bell. 11 months, black and white bitch, by Dash ex Crop, pupped August 10th 1835, not broken. 35 guineas to Mr Martyn.
10. A puppy 4 months old, by Regent ex Crop, pupped March 5th 1836. 15 guineas to Lord Douglas.
11. A puppy 4 months old, by Regent ex Crop, pupped March 5th 1836. 15 guineas to Mr Robertson.

Upon the death of the 5th Duke, the title became extinct and the estate passed to his nephew, the Duke of Richmond, who later became the Duke of Richmond and Gordon.

It is interesting that this Duke purchased Juno at the sale. He also bought a retriever called Diver, and another named Bess. It is generally accepted that, on taking over Gordon Castle, he revived the strain of setters, which by now had a remarkable reputation for good work, and put together a strong working kennel of Gordon Setters, as well as other gundogs.

George, the 5th Duke of Gordon. The title became extinct after his death.

'Gordon Setters in a Highland landscape,' signed and dated 1883, by Richard Andsell R.A. (1815-1885).

Although there are some conflicting reports, the principal colour seems to have been black, white and tan, with just a few black and tans, but the latter may have died out. This evidence is gleaned from the documentation at the closing of the Castle Kennel in 1907, when Isaac Sharpe, of the Stylish Gundog Kennels, bought all the remaining setters. We have evidence from him that these were all black, white and tan.

THE FIRST SHOW DOGS

The early setters were only bred to work. Their lineage was almost entirely dependent on the choices made by a good gamekeeper, with reference to his employer, of course. His very livelihood, which included his house, depended upon success in rearing and keeping a kennel of excellence for his master. Whether the colour of these setters was by choice, or whether the black and tans just happened to be better workers, is not known.

It was not recorded whether, in those early days, any of the Castle Setters were ever in any household other than the large kennels of an estate. It is unlikely they were kept as pets. In fact, in many ways, they were treated as Foxhound kennels are today. Any animal not considered to be one hundred per cent perfect was put down and it was not thought proper to give, or to be seen to have among the stock, any second-rate specimen. Therefore, it can be said, there is no record anywhere that one of this type of setter was kept as a pet.

Not until 1859, at Newcastle, do we hear of a show for dogs, and here a Gordon was awarded a first prize for Setters. This was Mr Jobling's Dandy. Later at Southill, in 1863, at the first-ever Field Trial, the first three places were awarded to Gordon Setters, which at that time were known as Black & Tans.

When the Kennel Club was first founded in 1873, the breed was officially classified as the Black and Tan Setter because it was well known that there were black and tan setters which had never had any connection with Gordon Castle and were not derived from any setter of that particular strain. It was in 1923 that the Kennel Club recognised Gordon Setters.

FURTHER DEVELOPMENTS

During the second half of the 19th century, the Rev. T. Pearce, who wrote under the nom-de-plume of "Idstone", had a most flourishing kennel of excellent Gordons. He lived at Morden Vicarage, Dorset. He is thought to be the purchaser of the male, Kent, who was a prolific sire, spreading his bloodline through many generations, but who was, unfortunately, a slightly flawed animal, in that he was a brilliant worker but had an ugly head.

The Rev. Pearce had ideas on dog keeping which were quite controversial compared to those of his contemporaries. He was the first to point out that dogs were much brighter than they were given credit for. He really loved his Gordons, caring greatly for their welfare and their comfort. In his writings, he points out that many setters, at the end of a shooting season, were simply returned to their kennels to live with other dogs as their sole companions and with very little human contact, let alone any human company, until the next shooting season. He refers to an 'educated' setter, taking care to point out that by this he does not mean gun-trained, and he writes: "I myself have had setters of marvellous sagacity, whose penetration into my intentions, whose reflections and method and deductions, have startled me at times and who acted from a power to which I should hesitate to give the name of instinct."

He tells the story of one of his Gordons, called Rhine, a bitch obtained from Mr Wemyss of Wemyss Castle. She was normally gentle and quiet in her kennel, but at the start of any preparation indicating that her master was going out shooting, she would scramble up her eight-foot kennel fence and get into his cart, without being seen. Several times she escaped notice until they had reached their destination, and once, after he had left, she tracked him over a distance of four miles and joined in the shoot, after announcing her arrival to her master, who was one of the guns.

Mr. Pearce also tells how Robin (Ranger ex Doll) was once out with a young retriever who missed a winged bird and was looking for it in vain. Although Robin was commanded to stay down, he got up, caught the running bird and took it to the retriever. Then he returned to the place where he had been given the command to drop, thereby proving his extreme intelligence in taking the bird to the retriever and not to his master.

Ch. Regent was probably Rev. Pearce's best Gordon, whom he had bred from the famous Argyle (owned by Lord Bolingbroke) out of the first bitch called Ruby (litter sister to Robin) in 1860, and who was jointly owned by Mr. Rowland Wood for a time. Ch. Kent was certainly the most famous dog he had. Regent was mated to Kent and produced, among others, Ch. Rex, Young Kent, La Reine, and Silk.

The opinion of Mr Pearce was often sought in any Gordon matters. He was greatly respected and seems to have been blessed with the gift of being able to see both the virtues and the faults in his own dogs. Towards the end of his dog breeding days, he said that Gordons were far too heavy and must be refined at all costs if the breed was to continue to be held in great esteem by other sportsmen. He seems to have been the first to realise this, yet he still maintained "I have seen better setters of the black and tan than any other breed."

One of Kent's great contemporaries was Brougham, bred and owned by Mr Burdett, a prominent landowner. He was from very different blood lines and was a convincing rival of Kent's but, although he was used with English, as well as with Gordon, setters, he never achieved the same popularity as Kent or served the same number of bitches. Kent became a legend in the breed and our present-day Gordons are saturated with his blood. Deeply as we may regret this inbreeding to what was an unsound dog in some ways, there is simply nothing we can do about it today. At the height of his popularity, it is said that he received about sixty bitches per year.

THE BREED CLUBS

It is not disputed that the patronage of the Dukes of Gordon, and their interest in developing a super working ability, brought these setters to fame and fashion, and so they continued to be popularly known as Gordon Setters. The Breed Clubs, founded in America in 1888 and in England in 1891, used this name. The fact that the Dukes lived in Scotland led to the breed being recognised as a native of that country.

At the turn of the century, the Gordon quickly gained favour with the more practical sportsman, who recognised the versatile ability of this dog. Although heavier at this time than other setters, the breed was well known for steadiness and long-lasting qualities. With the arrival of competitions, such as Field Trials, the Gordon became much in demand, for the dogs could be relied upon to produce satisfactory results, particularly on the Scottish grouse moors, where their strength and stamina were much in evidence.

THE START OF COMMERCIAL KENNELS

At the end of the 19th century and the beginning of the 20th, a great decline started in the large estates, which had been maintained by wealthy noblemen and landowners. At the same time, there came a surge in the establishment and growth of commercial kennels, where

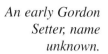

*An early Gordon
Setter, name
unknown.*

*A Gordon Setter
photographed in
the 1930s.*

many breeds of gundog were kept and hired out for shooting parties. One of these was the kennel of Isaac Sharpe. Evidence is at hand to give a good account of his activities, as his secretary, Margaret Dow, is still alive today and loves to relate many stories of how she had to arrange and manage his kennel whilst he was away with the dogs, trialling and selling.

Isaac Sharpe, who had acquired the very last of the 'Castle' setters, made his kennel into a Limited Company. It was probably the first commercial kennel. As well as many setters, he had Labradors, Springer Spaniels and some Pointers, numbering as many as two hundred during any one season. These dogs were hired out, sometimes for two weeks, often for the whole of the shooting season. Isaac Sharpe owned some 'shooting' of his own and it was part of his business to house shooting parties at local hostelries and hire his stock out, providing beaters and kennel boys to care for the dogs. The hiring fee for a setter was 12 guineas for Grouse, and this figure was constant, whether the dog went for two weeks, or for the whole season. His main kennel was at Douglas Brae but he did have another at Inglewood.

His business grew with the rise in popularity of the sporting aspect of shooting, so he took on staff. Margaret Dow joined him in 1925 with the keepers, Jamie King and John Brailsford, who trained the dogs. Together with three other trainers, they lived in a croft house on the edge of the moors, often accompanying dogs when they went out on hire.

Isaac Sharpe's affix was 'Stylish' and the Gordon section of his kennel held the best, hardy

This is believed to be Ch. Dawn of Daven (Peter of Crombie – Babs of Crombie), whelped in the 1930s. Dawn was a known producer of 'Red' Gordons.

dogs, capable of winning whenever they were shown and also giving a good account of themselves when worked, either in trials or merely shot over. The most brilliant was Stylish Ranger, who was born in 1900. His dam was an unregistered bitch called Fairy, his sire being Heather Crack. Ranger was notably the best Gordon Setter to run in public, but it was largely the superb handling by his owner, coupled with his excellent nose for game finding, that set him far ahead of others. It was said that Isaac Sharpe could 'put Ranger anywhere merely by the wave of a finger'.

It was not unusual for dogs to change hands many times during their active life and, in 1906, having won the Kennel Club Derby (1901) and the Kennel Club All Age Stake (1902), Ranger was exported to Norway. Yet William Arkwright, a writer of the day on canine matters, described him as 'a well made dog, too dark in colour and with a coarse head'. Ranger's son, Stylish Billie was said to be a 'beautiful breed type; good head and tan, stands on the best of legs and feet. Compact body. All through a grand specimen'. These were the words of J. Bishop, an eminent gundog judge; yet the only published photo of Billie shows him to be heavy in body and somewhat deficient in muzzle. Beauty in the eye of the beholder perhaps?

Isaac Sharpe died in 1938, just before the outbreak of World War II and also the year that Stylish Stagestruck won the Challenge Certificate at Cruft's, under Mrs D. Whitewell, who wrote: 'Stylish Stagestruck. A real sound young bitch with no trace of nerves. Her head is not true Gordon in character, but she has a grand neck, front body, hind leg, and is very sound. Went on to win the CC.' Shortly after this she joined the Blakeen Kennels of Mrs Sherman Hoyt in the United States, taking valuable Stylish blood across the Atlantic.

All the pedigrees in Gordon Setters today can be traced back, some to this kennel and others to the Castle Gordons. Peggy Grayson was so impressed with a present-day Gordon, Sh. Ch. Dudmoor Mylton of Lourdace, that she took the trouble to trace his lineage back to the Castle Gordons – His Grace the Duke of Gordon's Grouse (sire) and Nell (dam). This spans thirty generations.

Chapter Two

HEREDITY AND TEMPERAMENT

In order to understand the temperament of the Gordon Setter, it is a good idea first to take a look at hereditary elements. The family structure amongst animals is governed to some extent by the environment and will vary from species to species. Here we are only interested in the canine version and I am going to refer to the wonderful studies which have been made of the wolf.

THE ORIGINAL PATTERN
The wolf's pattern of behaviour can be applied to any breed of dog, although there will be variations in ferocity. The Gordon Setter, being a reticent creature, will not respond with the force and speed of one of the guarding breeds, which may be seen by some people to have a shorter 'fuse'!

When observing the wolf, it soon becomes noticeable that there are several males, and many females, all living in some kind of harmony together. This situation is the same with the African dog, which is probably the only surviving wild breed of dog in existence today. How then does this family come about, and how is its number controlled? Why is there no fighting and no great increase in the size of the family?

These questions are answered quite simply. Control is by way of a strong dominant male, known as the 'alpha' leader of this pack. The other noticeable feature is that there is also a top bitch, who may well turn out to become as aggressive as the top male, should the need arise. Mating is restricted to the alpha male and the top bitch only. The other males are too dominated by the alpha male to attempt to mate any other female that is around. The alpha female dominates the younger bitches. It is not known whether these young females do actually come into season or not. Certainly they receive no attention from any of the males present, at least not whilst the alpha male is present.

With the African dog, male members of the family join together with the young females to play, to hunt and even to share food with each other, although they quickly concede their place should either the alpha male or female come upon them. The alpha male will always feed first. He may share with the alpha female but not always. Then everyone joins in a free-for-all for the remainder of the meal.

Should any of the younger males attempt to mate with any of the bitches, he will be sharply admonished by the alpha male of the group and, should he persist, then there is a skirmish to determine who is to be respected. Should the youngster back off, then he will be allowed to stay, but should he persist, then the alpha male would have to either be so aggressive as to drive this intervener away or, at the very worst, kill him. This would be the only way that the top male could hold a position of respect. The day comes, of course, when the alpha male is too old to continue. In this situation the choice is the same – leave or die. As we are well aware, the rule in the wild is the survival of the fittest.

OWNING MALE DOGS

This pattern of behaviour shows the need for a 'top' dog or 'alpha' within a domestic situation, if life is to continue in harmony. Most dogs respond well to this situation, as it is part of their instinctive make-up. So, if you are the owner of a male, it may be that you have one with a temperament showing no wish to assert authority. If this is the case, then you will have a happy and contented companion for the length of his life; but if you have one who is destined to be a top dog, then it may be that you are not a strong enough personality to hold him down. There are certainly some people who should never own a male.

If you choose to own more than one male then, providing that the second one is acquired some years after the first one, there should be no problems, just as long as you remember that age usually decides who is boss and the younger one will be expected to grovel to his older companion. However, as a very young puppy, he will not have acquired this knowledge, as this is where his natural mother would play a large part. She would not allow him contact with any other adult until he knew his manners. This is where most humans fail. They mix these two together, usually with disastrous results. The new arrival is considered by the eldest to be invading his territory. The reaction is to growl in an effort to ward off this new and tiny intruder; but the pup sees the adult as being no different to his mother, who has always cosseted him. He does not understand the growl and continues to approach the older male who, when he cannot control the pup, bites him to ensure the youngster will leave him in peace.There are those Gordon owners who have allowed this to happen and, in spite of the subsequent need for intensive veterinary treatment for the pup, have continued, until the ultimate decision has to be made to keep them apart, never to meet again. The real answer to this problem is not to allow it to happen and then there is no need to find a cure. If, however, a cure is necessary then, once the pup has reached at least two years of age, allow them to meet on neutral territory, quite free and unrestrained by leads or the attention of people, and sort it out themselves. This may not be pleasant to watch, but dogs who have unfinished business will always be trying to get to one another for an aggressive confrontation until they have both ascertained who is top dog.

One can see from this the difficulties often encountered by owners trying to use a male at stud who is, quite possibly, dominated by the presence of an older male. This dominance may not be witnessed in any way, but it will be there. So many youngsters are accused of not being 'good studs' when this is not quite the case. It is rather that the younger male considers it is not his place to try to mate any bitch, because of his pecking order. When this occurred in my house, I sent my elder male to live with someone else as soon as the bitch that I had came into season. My young dog still remained an unwilling partner, until the bitch, at the peak of her season, made such a nuisance of herself that he did finally mate her. Should he

Aust. Ch.Trisetter Ebonie Dude, owned by Esther Joseph. It is important to understand how your dog's mind works.

be required to mate someone else's bitch then the answer is to take the dog to the bitch, otherwise the other male's scent would still be present and the youngster would assume that the older dog was still there.

CONTROLLING A BITCH

Bitches can be just as aggressive toward each other, with the elder one considering herself to be the alpha bitch, and that therefore the younger one should not be breeding. Trouble often arises when one or the other comes into season. I am fully aware of this and try to keep bitches of different ages apart when they are in season, as the youngsters are often bullied at this time. The way to prevent this pattern of behaviour is to get the eldest bitch spayed as soon as her breeding life is finished. This brings an end to her aggression towards the younger ones, although it can lead to skirmishes as the next bitch in the pecking order assumes her place.

UNDERSTANDING INSTINCTS

Knowledge of the hierarchy also helps in avoiding trouble within a home framework. We, the humans, do create most of the problems which occur with dogs, usually due to a lack of understanding of the great, powerful instincts that dogs are still carrying within their being. These instincts give them a code to live by, a code to survive with, and the interference of the humans is so often the cause of many difficulties.

By keeping more than two males, or more than two females, the human is breaking dog lore by wanting to use them all to breed with. So great care and thought must prevail. This, of course, only applies to those who live together in our homes, and not to those who spend their lives in kennels, where they are better living in pairs, with one of each sex sharing one kennel.

A bullying situation can arise when a bitch is spayed or a dog castrated. If either of these two were 'top' male or 'top' female prior to the neutering process, it is quite astounding how quickly roles can be reversed. I live with four males and four females, who all have a peaceful life together until either a younger bitch is bred from, or a younger male used at stud. I am the 'alpha' in this house; I do understand, and therefore can adjust to avoid problems. However, I did have cause to have my eldest bitch spayed. I made this decision because I did not wish to breed her again and an unnecessary season in this house is hard on the males. Although it has always been my policy to place the bitch who is in season into local kennels, there are times when all kennels are full, and she would have to stay at home. Hence the need to spay at the end of her breeding life, which for me, is three litters or twenty puppies. This particular bitch had spent years dominating her daughter. She was particularly hard on her when she herself was in whelp, and then meted out the same dominance when her daughter was in whelp. I had broken the pecking order by breeding the younger bitch. Yet, within four days of being spayed, the roles of these two were reversed. The younger bitch now put her mother in her place. She stood over her with her tail raised, as if in threat, and her mother accepted the situation without a murmur. Sometimes we humans find this very hard to get used to but, without interference on our part, this situation would not arise. What a lot we have to answer for!

RULES FOR PEACEFUL COHABITATION

To keep a peaceful household with all living together, there are a few other rules that I stick to and take heed of. One of these is the order of feeding. Although mine all have separate places in which to feed, I am very aware that there is a pecking order that must be adhered to. The top male is always fed first and so on down the order of the hierarchy. Similar rules apply when out walking. I have to have them all on leads together for some five hundred yards before I am clear of the main road and able to let everyone loose to gallop. My top male has a slightly longer lead than the others. This ensures that all the younger males are walking behind him which, of course, is their place.

I start the first exercise on a canal towpath and it is interesting to observe the younger males trying to find a means of getting ahead of the old dog. One chooses to duck into the adjacent field and emerge further along the towpath but the surprise he gets is quite astonishing, because the old boy is always there to chastise him for this behaviour. When we eventually get on to much wider spaces, then they are all busy doing their own thing, chasing rabbits and seeking out the odd brace of partridge to be found.

I never interfere with any admonishing the old boy decides upon, for this is the only way we are all to live in peace, and my interference would exacerbate an already dynamic situation. Sometimes the sounds of these chastisements are quite horrendous, yet there is never any bloodshed, no marks or scars, no visible damage at all. Each one knows exactly how far they can push their elders and betters! I have spoken to other owners of Gordons who, I know, dare not let their males meet at all, but it seems that they do not have the courage to put their house in order.

There is, however, a time when I do interfere and will not allow dog lore to prevail. That is when the old dog is about to be forced to relinquish 'alpha' position. This would be hard for me to witness. I would be watching an old dog taking a beating day after day while the younger and more virile male took over. As a human being, my own feelings could not allow this, so I then separate the oldies. I usually have a dog and a bitch of similar ages, so these two then walk separately from the youngsters; they don't need to go so far and love the time to amble and explore at their own pace. They also sleep a lot and spend more time lounging around. I keep them separate by the use of indoor kennels which are like large cages.

CHARACTERISTICS OF THE GORDON SETTER

The dictionary gives the meaning of the word temperament as: 'individual character of one's physical constitution permanently affecting the manner of acting, feeling and thinking'.

When people refer to temperament when speaking of dogs, it is usually to remark that the animal has a good or bad temperament. This, as with many others things, very much depends upon what each individual expects from their relationship with their dog. A bad temperament may well be taken to mean that a dog bites, whilst the opposite – a good temperament – could imply that the animal is friendly. These statements have very vague interpretations when we consider the animal and the inborn instincts governing actions and behaviour. I prefer to use the word 'behaviour' rather than 'temperament'.

Living with any dog, not only a Gordon Setter, requires an acceptable level of behaviour from that animal. It is very sad that many dogs lose their credibility and, indeed, in some

Clanset Gordon Setters: Dogs must learn to live together in harmony.

cases their lives, because their behaviour is not acceptable to society. This is not always the animal's fault. It may be a case of just following instinct or of being in a bad environment. In most cases of bad behaviour, humans are the responsible party, although they may be unaware of the part they have played in developing the situation.

Were Gordons still able to live in their own hierarchy, in the wild and uninterrupted by human beings, it is my belief that they would stay in a family group. They would remain with their mother until they were nine to ten months of age. She would be responsible for everything they learned. She would also have some control over their experiences, their diet and their behaviour. However, this situation does not exist for any canine now living in our society. Puppies are bred and removed from their dams at eight and sometimes six weeks of age. Whoever takes them on at this stage of their development also takes on the responsibility for the puppy's education. Without a mother, who will let this puppy know what behaviour is acceptable and what is not? The puppy becomes reliant on the owners for food, a place to sleep, exercise, socialising, travel, everything. How much will the new owner work hard to achieve and how much will be left to this youngster to work out alone?

TAKING RESPONSIBILITY
Gordon Setters are, by nature, a reticent breed, not liable to fight, not even to have confrontations of any kind, no matter with whom. Given a choice, which on many occasions they are not, Gordons would walk away, even if the manner in which they did so caused loss of face.

It is a good thing for us humans to reflect upon the situations where we give the Gordon no choice, often causing confrontations when our dog would rather avoid them. Out on walks, when on the leash, causes the most problems. This situation can arise so many times, at shows, where the Gordon must behave, or suffer remonstration for not complying with the owner's wishes, causing much embarrassment. It also occurs at training sessions and when attending Field Trials, where the lead is kept on until the turn comes for running.

We really do pressurise our canine friends, sometimes beyond their endurance. So how are we to teach youngsters to ensure that what we refer to as a good temperament will develop? This has to be given some careful thought because, if your dog has been purchased as a show specimen, then you will need an outgoing character. It is detrimental to have one who is too reticent.

RESPECTING YOUR DOG
We must be aware that a Gordon Setter is not a child. Many owners treat their dogs as children and, in some cases, the dog becomes the child they never had, or replaces children who have now left the nest for homes and families of their own.

Gordons, indeed any dogs, are not children and should never be treated as such. They are animals with a 'lore' of their own by way of many inbred instincts, which they will follow. A dog has no imagination, and only knows the present time. There is no knowledge of yesterday or that there will be a tomorrow. Reactions are really recollections from the memory bank. This will have stored sights, sounds, feelings, noises, comfort and pain and it is these experiences which control behaviour to owners and to others of the animal kingdom,

Your Gordon Setter has many inbred instincts which you must respect.

as and when they occur. Dogs follow a routine well – in fact this is how they learn and thrive, remaining constant, usually in contentment. Having no imagination, it is patterns that are learned and followed. For example, if one procedure terminates in feeding, then every time this procedure is followed, the dog will become excited at the expectation of food. If putting on wellingtons precedes a walk, then even picking up the wellingtons may result in similar excitement to walking, even if the owner is only going into the garden.

A similar situation arises in my house. I exercise my dogs wearing a leather pair of walking boots. To try to get these on to my feet with the dogs milling all around, barking and charging about, is impossible. I live in a quiet urban area and these goings-on would very soon make me extremely unpopular with my neighbours. So, to keep the dogs quiet, I take my boots with me into the bathroom, so as not to have witnesses to my boot procedure. This way I emerge ready for the exercise and with very little time for my dogs to realise what is going to happen.

Dogs who have been used to working with accompanying noises from a gun, will immediately raise their ears and look expectantly around at the sound of a car back-firing, or some similar noise. I once had a bitch who had been shot over and loved gun work and, as we live quite close to a road, would display this behaviour at banging sounds; yet she was terrified of thunder and could differentiate between the two.

REASONS FOR BAD BEHAVIOUR

It is my belief that there are two main reasons for bad temperament, or bad behaviour. These are a lack of socialisation when very young, and owners who have allowed their puppy to learn alone, without being given any protection. The result is that the puppy either gets bitten by other dogs or is punished for committing what, in the owner's eyes, is a sin but in the puppy's view is normal behaviour. Puppies learn very quickly, and attention is something they seek and need. One must remember that bad attention, and by that I mean smacking, is better than no attention at all, in the eyes of the pup.

Many owners *teach* their puppies to behave badly by simply allowing it to happen. These owners never allow a puppy to learn what is acceptable and what is not. The owner may think it cute when the puppy comes and drops a ball in his lap. Little do they know that the puppy is demanding their attention, and getting it. When the puppy is older such dominance may be demonstrated in a very different way. Only play with the puppy when you want to, never when it is demanded of you. A puppy stealing from a table needs to be told that this is not puppy territory and such behaviour is not allowed. I have witnessed some owners who have simply made excuses such as "Well, I suppose I shouldn't have left it there." When that puppy is an adult there may be problems when food is stolen from the table by an alpha who assumes the food there is a right.

I have a friend who suffered similar behaviour and still went on making excuses for the dog but never remonstrating, whatever the offence. This ended rather sadly when the dog decided that he was the alpha in this house and was going to remind all the occupants, at different times, of his position. He almost removed his owner's fingers over what appeared, on the surface, to be nothing. This behaviour may well be fine in the dog pack but it is totally unacceptable in our society and the dog was put down. His death caused a lot of grief, for whatever he had done, he was dearly loved. The owner, although realising much later that she had encouraged this behaviour, now has another dog and, sadly, is doing the same things all over again.

GAINING UNDERSTANDING

Physical abuse is not necessary to attain the top position in your own house; just a little knowledge of what an animal's undomesticated lifestyle would be is helpful. The study of wildlife, and how to make it work satisfactorily for us, is not difficult and is only really common sense.

To understand how the animal kingdom works with regard to dogs, we really have to make a study of their actions when they are in their own territory, either that of the wolf, who really is just another breed of dog, or that of the wild dogs that still exist in Africa. Until recently the wolf was still visible in parts of Canada and some parts of Europe. There have been many studies made and lengthy articles written about the wolf, and I use these as part of the teaching for my behaviour lectures and explanations of why sometimes things go wrong.

Some years ago, someone introduced wolves to a part of Scotland so as to study behaviour and lifestyle. The man in question went to a vast amount of expense in erecting eight-foot chain-linked fencing around a whole forest so as to make escape for these wolves impossible. Sadly, the local population, on discovering what he had done, panicked, imagining all sorts of disasters, and cut the fencing, allowing the wolves to escape. They knew that this action would mean intervention on the part of the police and the result was a hunt by helicopter and death from a bullet. However, although the end was tragic and caused the project to be abandoned, there was time for much information to be stored both on paper and by way of videos. I have seen the videos and use their findings in my teaching.

In spite of many stories about wolves and their methods of gaining food there has never been any truth in those tales which involve wolves hunting and killing man. This is a fact. Certainly it is known that wolves did follow people, especially the lone traveller, but it was more likely to have been for the food scraps which were left behind rather than for the human flesh to eat!

The Gordon Setter is similar in behaviour. Left alone, the dog will be able to make choices but, if invited to share our home, then we need to teach the dog in the same way that a mother would, were she still around. We take on this role when we take home that small bundle and we must honour our obligation.

If your pup is behaving in such a way that a reminder needs to be issued about who is the boss, beating is not the answer. Merely simulate what the dominant male would do – and that is, grab the offender by the scruff of the neck, give a bit of a shake while making growling noises, then place the miscreant down on on the floor and make eye contact until the puppy looks away. Then step over the top and walk away.

Chapter Three

BREED STANDARDS

THE REASON FOR BREED STANDARDS

Breed Standards are important because they ensure that, with the passing of time, the breed appearance does not change in any way. Otherwise there could be a loss of type, with variability of height, coat, and colour, throughout the breed. Indeed it could then happen that the breed would no longer be recognisable, because each animal would be different in appearance.

Breed Standards were first written down at the beginning of this century, after the Kennel Club had become well established and shows were starting to take place with regularity. Prior to this time, the importance of keeping a dog, especially a gundog, was the ability to work, either for the sporting gentlemen of the day or for the poorer members of society, such as the poacher who needed his dog to catch his dinner. Whatever the needs of the owner, it was essential that the dog be fit and able to work, hence the breed Standards came to be written to describe the dogs which represented their breeds at that time and were useful workers.

THE NECESSITY FOR PROPER CONFORMATION

For anyone, either a person or an animal, to use their body to advantage, it is required that the bone structure and conformation are correct. By the word correct, we mean built in such a way that movement is easy, comfortable, and tireless. Of course, the animal, or man, will also require inbuilt stamina, but it is the dog with which we are concerned.

This is why shoulder angulation should equal the angulation involved with the rear assembly of the dog, and the reason for feet being correctly structured. This is also the reason for heart and lung room. The functioning of any live being depends upon its structure, as does its ability to perform tirelessly. To enable a dog to work all day, to hunt, to use every hunting instinct and not tire was important, and the Standards are laid down to ensure that this animal continues to survive.

DIFFERENCES BETWEEN STANDARDS

The Standards referred to here are applicable to the Gordon Setter and, while it is quite true that the statements made within each Standard mean the same, or similar, attributes, there are subtle differences, the main difference being that of the American Gordon. In the American Standard a greater allowance has been made for height, and weight, and the proportions of

The judge must use the Standard to find the best representatives of the breed. I had the honour of judging Gordon Setters at Crufts 1994. Pictured left is my dog CC winner, Sh. Ch. Carek Ebony Tusker (who also took Best Of Breed), owned by Yvonne Horrocks, handled by her son, Derek. The bitch CC winner was Sh. Ch. Wallbank Sweet Success, owned and handled by Angela Backler.

foreface to the distance from the stop to the occiput, while the UK Standard requires a shorter distance from muzzle to stop than from stop to occiput. The American Standard also mentions a sloping topline, where the UK prefers a fairly short, level back.

The Standard used by the British Gordon Setter Club is the one which was in place before the Kennel Club demanded it be made more concise. The Standard which was then imposed upon the breed club was such that it totally distorted the rugged appearance of the Gordon and was found to be unacceptable. To date, the KC has not changed its mind – but neither has the British Gordon Setter Club!

It is the Australians that come out top in my estimation as, although they use the British Standard, they have illustrated it, so that the actual part of the structure mentioned can be seen, and must leave an impression on those who read it and compare it with the present-day Gordon. After all, interpretation of these Standards will not be the same for each person. Therefore the Gordon Setter Club of New South Wales has added to their pictorial Standard by embellishing the meaning of each paragraph, and I have used this excellent version, following a reproduction of the British and American Breed Standards. You will also note that they do not refer to any faults at all. This is quite deliberate, as it is believed that to learn the faults in any breed may well lead to fault judging. The Standard used in the European countries is the same as in the UK but is translated into the language of each country.

POINTS OF ANATOMY

Illustrated by Sh. Ch. Breightonside Dark Avenger.

CLEAR STOP

FAIRLY HEAVY HEAD,
FINELY CHISELLED

STRAIGHT OR SLIGHTLY WAVED COAT,
NOT CURLY

DARK EYE

MODERATELY SLOPING TOPLINE

LOW SET EARS

NECK LONG, LEAN, ARCHED

SHOULDERS DEEP, SLOPING, WELL BACK

CLOSE COUPLED, FAIRLY SHORT BODY

TAIL CARRIED NEARLY HORIZONTALLY

DEEP, SQUARE
MUZZLE

WITHOUT
THROATINESS

CHEST DEEP,
NOT TOO BROAD

LONG, FLAT,
MUSCULAR

FORELEGS BIG BONED
AND STRAIGHT

RIBS WELL SPRUNG

ELBOWS FREE, WELL
LET DOWN

FULL TOE PADS,
DEEP HEEL CUSHIONS

STIFLE AND HOCK JOINTS WELL BENT,
INCLINED NEITHER IN NOR OUT

HOCKS
SHORT,
STRONG

BRITISH BREED STANDARD

GENERAL APPEARANCE
Stylish dog, with galloping lines, consistent with its build which can be compared to a weight-carrying hunter. Symmetrical in conformation throughout.

CHARACTERISTICS
Intelligent, able and dignified.

TEMPERAMENT
Bold, outgoing, of a kindly, even disposition.

THE HEAD
Head deep rather than broad, but broader than muzzle, showing brain room. Skull slightly rounded, broadest between ears. Clearly defined stop; length from occiput to stop longer than from stop to nose. Below and above eyes lean, cheeks as narrow as leanness of head allows. Muzzle long with almost parallel lines, neither pointed, nor snipey. Flews not pendulous, clearly defined lips. Nose large, broad, nostrils open and black, Muzzle not quite as deep as its length.

EYES
Dark brown, bright. Neither deep nor prominent, set sufficiently under brows, showing keen, intelligent expression.

EARS
Medium size, thin, set low, lying close to head.

MOUTH
Jaws strong with a perfect, regular and complete scissor bite, i.e. upper teeth closely overlapping the lower teeth and set square to the jaws.

NECK
Long, lean, arched, without throatiness.

FOREQUARTERS
Shoulder blades long, sloping well back, wide flat bone, close at withers, not loaded. Elbows well let down and close to the body. Forelegs flat-boned, straight, strong upright pasterns.

THE BODY
Moderate length, deep brisket, ribs well sprung, back ribs deep, loins wide, slightly arched, chest not too broad.

HINDQUARTERS
From hip to hock long, broad and muscular, hock to heel short, strong, stifles well bent, straight from hock joint to ground. Pelvis tending to horizontal.

FEET
Oval, close knit, well arched toes, plenty of hair between. Well padded toes, deep heel cushions.

TAIL
Straight or slightly scimitar, not reaching below hocks. Carried horizontally or below line of back. Thick at root, tapering to fine point. Feather or flag starting near root, long, straight, growing shorter to point.

GAIT/MOVEMENT
Steady, free moving and true, plenty of drive behind.

COAT
On head, front of legs, tops of ears short and fine, moderate length, flat and free from curl or wave on all other parts of body. Feather on upper portion of ears long and silky, on backs of legs long, fine, flat and straight; fringes on belly may extend to chest and throat. As free as possible from curl or wave.

COLOUR
Deep shining coal black, without rustiness, with markings of chestnut red, i.e. lustrous tan. Black pencilling on toes and black streak under jaw permissible. "Tan markings": two clear spots over eyes not over 2cm (3/4in) in diameter; on sides of muzzle, tan not reaching above base of nose, resembling a stripe around clearly defined end of muzzle from one side to other. Also on throat, two large, clear spots on chest. On inside hindlegs and inside thighs, showing down front of stifle and broadening out to outside of hindlegs from hock to toes; on forelegs, up to elbows behind, and to knees or a little above, in front; around vent. Very small white spot on chest permissible. No other colour permissible.

SIZE
Height: dogs: 66 cms (26 ins); bitches: 62 cms (24.1/2 ins). Weight: dogs: 29.5kgs (65lbs); bitches: 25.5kgs (56lbs).

FAULTS
Any departure from the foregoing points should be considered a fault and the seriousness with which the fault should be regarded should be in exact proportion to its degree.

NOTE: Male animals should have two apparently normal testicles fully descended into the scrotum.

Reproduced by kind permission of The Kennel Club.

Am. Can. Ch. Sassenach National Rendezvous: A Group and Specialty winner. Owned and bred by Judith Brown.

Mikron Photos.

GORDON SETTER CLUB OF AMERICA
STANDARD AND DESCRIPTION OF THE GORDON SETTER

GENERAL APPEARANCE
The Gordon Setter is a good sized, sturdily built, black and tan dog, well muscled, with plenty of bone and substance, but active, upstanding and stylish, appearing capable of doing a full day's work in the field. He has a strong, rather short back, with well-sprung ribs and a short tail. The head is fairly heavy and finely chiseled. His bearing is intelligent, noble, and dignified, showing no signs of shyness or viciousness. Clear colours and straight or slightly waved coat are correct. He suggests strength and stamina rather than extreme speed. Symmetry and quality are most essential. A dog well-balanced in all points is preferable to one with outstanding good qualities and defects. A smooth, free movement, with high head carriage, is typical.

SIZE, PROPORTION, SUBSTANCE
Size – Shoulder height for males, 24 to 27 inches; females, 23 to 26 inches. Weight for

males, 55 to 80 pounds; females, 45 to 70 pounds. Animals that appear to be over or under the prescribed weight limits are to be judged on the basis of conformation and condition. Extremely thin or fat dogs are discouraged on the basis that under or overweight hampers the true working ability of the Gordon Setter. The weight-to-height ratio makes him heavier than other Setters.

Proportion – The distance from the forechest to the back of the thigh is approximately equal to the height from the ground to the withers.
The Gordon Setter has plenty of bone and substance.

HEAD
Head deep, rather than broad, with plenty of brain room. Eyes – of fair size, neither too deep-set, not too bulging, dark brown, bright and wise. The shape is oval rather than round. The lids are tight. Ears – set low on the head approximately on line with the eyes, fairly large and thin, well folded and carried close to the head. Skull – nicely rounded, good-sized, broadest between the ears. Below and above the eyes is lean, and the cheeks as narrow as the leanness of the head allows. The head should have a clearly indicated stop. Muzzle – fairly long and not pointed, either as seen from above or from the side. The flews are not pendulous. The muzzle is the same length as the skull from occiput to stop and the top of the muzzle is parallel to the line of the skull extended. Nose – broad, with open nostrils, and black in color. The lip line from the nose to the flews shows a sharp, well-defined, square contour. Teeth – strong and white, meeting in front in a scissors bite, with the upper incisors slightly forward of the lower incisors. A level bite is not a fault. Pitted teeth from distemper or allied infections are not penalized.

NECK, TOPLINE, BODY
Neck – long, lean, arched to the head, and without throatiness. Topline – moderately sloping. Body – short from shoulder to hips. Chest – deep and not too broad in front; the ribs well-sprung, leaving plenty of lung room. The chest reaches to the elbows. A pronounced forechest is in evidence. Loins – short and broad and not arched. Croup – nearly flat, with only a slight slope to the tailhead. Tail – short and not reaching below the hocks, carried horizontal or nearly so, not docked, thick at the root and finishing in a fine point. The placement of the tail is important for correct carriage. When the angle of the tail bends too sharply at the first coccygeal bone, the tail will be carried too gaily or will droop. The tail placement is judged in relationship to the structure of the croup.

FOREQUARTERS
Shoulders – fine at the points, and laying well back. The tops of the shoulder blades are close together. When viewed from behind, the neck appears to fit into the shoulders in smooth, flat lines that gradually widen from neck to shoulder. The angle formed by the shoulder blade and upper arm bone is approximately 90 degrees when the dog is standing so that the foreleg is perpendicular to the ground. Forelegs – big-boned, straight and not bowed, with elbows free and not turned in or out. Pasterns are straight.

Dew-claws may be removed. Feet – cat-like in shape, formed by close-knit, well-arched toes with plenty of hair between; with full toe pads and deep heel cushions. Feet are not turned in or out.

HINDQUARTERS

The hind legs from hip to hock are long, flat and muscular; from hock to heel, short and strong. The stifle and hock joints are well bent and not turned either in or out. When the dog is standing with the rear pastern perpendicular to the ground the thigh bone hangs downward parallel to an imaginary line drawn upward from the hock. Feet as in front.

THE COAT

Soft and shining, straight or slightly waved, but not curly, with long hair on ears, under stomach and on chest, on back of the fore and hind legs, and on the tail. The feather which starts near the root of the tail is slightly waved or straight, having a triangular appearance, growing shorter uniformly toward the end.

COLOR AND MARKINGS

Black with tan markings, either of rich chestnut or mahogany color. Black pencilling is allowed on the toes. The borderline between black and tan colors is clearly defined. There are not any tan hairs mixed in the black. The tan markings are located as follows: (1) Two clear spots over the eyes and not over three-quarters of an inch in diameter; (2) On the sides of the muzzle. The tan does not reach to the top of the muzzle, but resembles a stripe around the end of the muzzle from one side to the other; (3) On the throat; (4) Two large clear spots on the chest; (5) On the inside of the hind legs showing down the front of the stifle and broadening out to the outside of the hind legs from the hock to the toes. It must not completely eliminate the black on the back of the hind legs; (6) On the forelegs from the carpus, or a little above, downward to the toes; (7) Around the vent; (8) A white spot on the chest is allowed, but the smaller the better. Predominantly tan, red or buff dogs which do not have the typical pattern of markings of a Gordon Setter are ineligible for showing and undesirable for breeding.

GAIT

A bold, strong, driving free-swinging gait. The head is carried up and the tail 'flags' constantly while the dog is in motion. When viewed from the front the forefeet move up and down in straight lines so that the shoulder, elbow and pastern joints are approximately in line. When viewed from the rear, the hock, stifle and hip joints are approximately in line. Thus the dog moves in a straight pattern forward without throwing the feet in or out. When viewed from the side the forefeet are seen to lift up and reach forward to compensate for the driving hindquarters. The hindquarters reach well forward and stretch far back enabling the stride to be long and the drive powerful. The overall appearance of the moving dog is one of smooth-flowing, well-balanced rhythm, in which the action is pleasing to the eye, effortless, economical and harmonious.

TEMPERAMENT
The Gordon Setter is alert, gay, interested, and aggressive. He is fearless and willing, intelligent and capable. He is loyal and affectionate, and strong-minded enough to stand the rigors of training.

DISQUALIFICATION
Predominantly tan, red or buff dogs which do not have the typical pattern of markings of a Gordon Setter.

Approved October 9th, 1990.

EXTENSION TO THE BRITISH BREED STANDARD

Prepared by the Gordon Setter Club of New South Wales, Australia.

The Gordon Setter is a unique dog and, as such, has certain characteristics which are unique to the breed.

Very often judges who are not specialists in a breed may not be aware of the particular idiosyncrasies of that breed. The first and general impression they get from a breed is that instant sighting in a ring, a limited time to get the general appearance details. This should convey many vital and important qualities. The viewer must know what to look for, and it helps to have a simple and efficient way to assess the dog.

The whole shape and outline of the dog should be considered, while trying to ignore possible distortion by a luxurious and profuse coat.

One of the most important features of the Gordon is its distinctive build. A Gordon that looks like a black and tan Irish or English Setter is not built correctly and therefore is not typical of the breed.

It is important to get the "feel" for the correct shape and proportions of the Gordon, to "know" just what balances and what is a little extreme, or perhaps "out of balance". A dog that is totally satisfying aesthetically, and which meets the requirements for the breed, is indicative of true TYPE.

The Gordon should have a noble, elegant head carriage. His head should have refined chiselling. The neck is long, arched, held at an angle of about the 10.30 position. His expression should be dignified, noble and intelligent. His movement should be agile. In no way should he be likened to a heavy, slow work-horse. The section of the Standard on General Appearance does not mention colour, which is left to another part, but it is necessary to know initially that the Gordon is a black and tan dog.

GENERAL APPEARANCE
"Stylish dog, with galloping lines, consistent with its build which can be compared to a weight-carrying hunter. Symmetrical in conformation throughout."
"Stylish dog". The first word of the Gordon Setter Standard says a great deal. Webster's

Sh. Ch. Gladstone of Lourdace (left) and Sh. Ch. Lourdace Graph Spae winning the 'double' at Bournemouth Championship Show in 1988. Gladstone took the award for Best of Breed. In his career he won a total of twenty-seven CCs, and was top winning Gordon Setter in 1987 and 1988.

David Dalton.

Dictionary defines style as "Mode or manner which is deemed elegant or in accord with a Standard ..." and again "The quality which gives distinctive excellence to artistic expression...".

"Consistent with its build which can be compared to a weight-carrying hunter". The reference in the Standard to a horse, in this case a weight-carrying hunter, is particularly apt with regards to the Gordon Setter.

There is little difference in the height of the racing thoroughbred (the Irish Setter?) and the weight-carrying hunter – itself usually a thoroughbred; the difference lies in the substance of the animal. The weight-carrying hunter must be able to go all day carrying a heavy rider. He is therefore capacious in chest and lung room, strong and well muscled in loin, with solidly boned legs and, most important, he is completely sound. These requirements should also apply to the Gordon Setter.

"Symmetrical in conformation throughout". The previous Standard added more detail to this, thus: "showing true balance. Strong fairly short and level back, Shortish tail. Head fairly long". Symmetry in conformation is essential. The dog must show "true balance". Trueness is the correct formation and angles of the frame. The frame of a dog should be true. The limbs must be vertical uprights in support, when viewed from the front, or rear. The movement should also show a trueness of direction, and limbs must not have any deviation in construction that will interfere with this true locomotion.

Balance and symmetry also demand that all parts of the dog would fit together harmoniously. The head should not be too heavy for the body, the neck should have the length to carry the head in a noble and aristocratic way, the front end should match the back in strength and substance, angles and lengths of limbs should compare with each other. The total dog should consist of qualities that blend so that they belong to the whole. It should never look as though one part could belong to another animal.

The symmetry and balance are of course applicable to the mature Gordon. It should be noted that the Gordon is a very slow maturing dog and therefore young Gordons up to the age of two to three years may not have achieved their final balance. It is common for young Gordons to grow unevenly, so that the legs may be out of balance with the body. This should be borne in mind when assessing young dogs.

CHARACTERISTICS
"Intelligent, able and dignified".
Do not forget that the Gordon was developed as a working gundog. He has to use his nose, brains, and common sense. He has to have the **"intelligence"** to recognise and obey commands of all kinds. His intelligence is one of the assets that make him an endearing companion. The Gordon's intelligence makes him a good obedience dog and there have been many with obedience titles.

The **"ableness"** required encompasses his sensing ability and physical build for his work. This, of course, requires him to be a sound dog. Therefore soundness is one of the bases on which a judge must assess his worth.

The Gordon is **"dignified"**, with a quiet and reserved demeanour. These are qualities which distinguish him from the other setters. He does not go willingly to every stranger, and may appear quite aloof in the ring. This however does not suggest that he should back off, or show shyness.

TEMPERAMENT
"Bold, outgoing, of a kindly even disposition".
"Bold" and **"outgoing"** are qualities which are best in evidence when working in the field. Here the Gordon should be alert and ready for action, and persistent even when the terrain is adverse.

A **"kindly even disposition"** is expected and is very obvious in the way he works in the field and by the loyalty and devotion he gives to his "family".

THE HEAD
"Head deep rather than broad, but broader than muzzle, showing brain room. Skull slightly rounded, broadest between ears. Clearly defined stop; length from occiput to stop longer than from stop to nose. Below and above eyes lean, cheeks as narrow as leanness of head allows. Muzzle long with almost parallel lines, neither pointed, nor snipey. Flews not pendulous, clearly defined lips. Nose large, broad, nostrils open and black, Muzzle not quite as deep as its length."

The head is a VERY important feature influencing not only the physical appearance of the dog, but also its perceived character. It should give an immediate impression of a NOBLE and STRONG dog.

Today's Standard actually describes the overall shape and size of the head very well but the

Male head study:
Sh. Ch. Inkersall
Curlew.

Bert & Mary Dyde.

statements are disjointed, so first we will discuss all the statements relating to the dimensions of the head.

"Head deep rather than broad, but broader than muzzle. Skull slightly rounded, broadest between ears, length from occiput to stop longer than from stop to nose. Muzzle long with almost parallel lines.... not quite as deep as its length."

The Gordon Head was described by Frank Warner Hill, the UK Gundog expert, in 1975, thus: "should come towards making him the most noble looking and strongest of the Setter group. To a considerable extent it should be his dominating feature (other than his colour) squarely constructed both in skull and foreface, and particularly in foreface, like a brick. Long, square and not overwide." The skull should be SLIGHTLY rounded, NOT "dome" shaped or flat.

"Broadest between the ears". The skull when viewed from above is slightly rounded (with furrow between eyes) and should not be pear or wedge shaped.

The relationship between length and depth of the head is fairly well defined. However, the width is of equal importance. The Standard states "showing brain room". Therefore the head should not be narrow or weak.

"Muzzle long with almost parallel lines". The muzzle should have almost parallel lines

Female head study: Sh. Ch. Lourdace Bridoon.   *Gibbs.*

when viewed from top and side. The top of the muzzle should be level, NOT concave or down turned.

"Neither pointed nor snipey". The muzzle should suggest a strong jaw and be able to accommodate a well-developed nose and nasal passages to aid the dog's keen scenting ability. The front of the muzzle should be square, when viewed from above.

"Cheeks as narrow as leanness of head allows". The cheek bones should be flat and not prominent – prominent cheek bones promote undesirable coarseness: this can be recognised by an angular protruding transition from skull to muzzle below the eyes (the zygomatic arch).

"Below and above eyes lean". There should be no excess flesh above or below the eyes as this leads to the "Bloodhound" look and hawy eyes which are definitely undesirable.

"Clearly defined stop". A clearly defined stop complements the definite brow.

"Flews not pendulous, clearly defined lips". The flews should not hang far below the line of the lower jaw, the desired squareness of muzzle coming from correct jaws configuration, not over-developed flews.

"Nose large, broad, nostrils open and black". To allow for good passage of air through to the scent organs, to promote good scenting power. These features are required to give the desired strong square muzzle. No colour other than black is acceptable.

Common deviations from the desired head include heads that are pointed in the muzzle and snipey or conversely muzzles that have heavy drooping flews. As a rough guide, the muzzle should not be quite as deep as its length. Overly broad and flat skulls are undesirable, as are excessively narrow skulls or those that are overly rounded.

Correct markings on the head are a major factor in the appearance of the dog.

EYES

"Dark brown, bright. Neither deep nor prominent, set sufficiently under brows, showing keen, intelligent expression".

The eye colour is ideally a lustrous dark brown which is not always easy to obtain. Suffice it to say, the darker the eye colour, the better. A yellow eye is most unattractive in a Gordon. The set of the eye influences its size and shape. The correct shape of the eye, which is not mentioned in the Standard, is normally considered to be oval. A staring round or "bug eye" will result from a prominent eye set, which will be more susceptible to damage. Deep-set eyes will tend to be smaller than desired and may lead to some restriction in vision.

Haw eye and accompanying loose skin give rise to a "Bloodhound" expression and also to problems with foreign objects entering the eye.

Some additional protection to the eye should be afforded by being set under well-defined brows.

EARS

"Medium size, thin, set low, lying close to head". The ear set should be approximately level with the eyes. High-set ears detract from the elegance of the head and are therefore undesirable. Thin ears are desirable, as thicker ears are of course heavier and may lead to ear troubles, as well as spoiling the appearance of the dog.

"Lying close to head" to protect against intrusion of foreign objects.

MOUTH
"Jaws strong with a perfect, regular and complete scissor bite, i.e. upper teeth closely overlapping the lower teeth and set square to the jaws."
The mouth should have a scissor bite. Complete dentition is desirable.

NECK
"Long, lean, arched, without throatiness". The neck should be long, lean, arched to the head, without throatiness, flowing smoothly into well-laid shoulders. Overly short neck and upright lay of shoulder result in an abrupt change in angle between the neck and the back instead of a nice smooth line and are therefore undesirable. Remember that the Standard calls for symmetrical conformation; extreme length, or shortness are undesirable.

Throatiness in a mature dog is undesirable, spoiling the line of the neck. A tendency towards throatiness can sometimes be seen in youngsters which may disappear as the dog matures.

FOREQUARTERS
"Shoulder blades long, sloping well back, wide flat bone, close at withers, not loaded. Elbows well let down and close to the body. Forelegs flat-boned, straight, strong upright pasterns".
It must be noted that the Gordon Setter was developed over a long period of time, to work over a specific terrain. The Gordon has long sloping shoulders, flat bone with strong legs and upright pasterns, to enable the dog to work through the heavy heather-covered, often steep and rocky moors. The other Setter breeds were designed to work over more open, less rugged terrains and this is reflected in their different construction.

The shoulders (scapula) should be long and slope well back, with wide flat bone close at the withers. The upper arm (humerus) should be long and well angulated at the point of shoulder (where the shoulder blade and upper arm meet).

Closeness at the withers is relative to the size of the dog. There must be space between the shoulder blades to allow for freedom of action. Because of the heavier build of the Gordon, the space between the shoulder blades at the withers should be wider than that of the other Setter breeds. The perpendicular from the withers should drop through the elbows to the back of the pasterns.

Loaded shoulders refers to the overdevelopment of muscle around the scapula. This usually occurs with incorrect shoulder or upper arm construction.

It is the length of shoulder and upper arm and the correct angulation together with the correct depth of body that allows the elbows to show below the body which gives the effortless ground-covering movement which must be striven for.

The flat bone of the forelegs is more obvious to the eye than that of the shoulder. Round bone as found in the English Setter should be penalised. The bone of the leg should be strong but not coarse, extending through to the pasterns. Too heavy bone lends to clumsy movement. Bone that is too coarse or is too fine is uncharacteristic.

The pasterns (metacarpus) are the shock absorbers of the front assembly. They should be strong and upright., However, because of the work the Gordon is required to do, a slight angle is required.

The pastern is not as upright or as short as is seen, for example, in the Harrier or the Foxhound. Conversely, too much slope of pastern would be seen as a weakness.

As the Gordon Setter is an air scenting breed, working on heavy, uneven terrain, a strong deep shoulder construction, strong bone and good feet are essential.

THE BODY

"Moderate length, deep brisket, ribs well sprung, back ribs deep, loins wide, slightly arched, chest not too broad".

"Moderate Length". It is very hard to describe the term "moderate". As quoted above from the Dictionary, it means "avoiding extremes...".

There may seem to be some contradiction between a moderate length and the desirable feature of a fairly short back, but actually when considering the body in detail both can be considered correct.

The length of the body is measured from the point of buttock to the point of shoulder. The height of the dog is measured from the top of the withers to the ground. In order that the back legs should not interfere with the front when moving, the length should be slightly longer than the height; this then gives the body its moderate length.

The back length is usually taken to be from the withers to the pelvis. If the dog has a correctly angled pelvis and well laid back shoulders, this length is short in comparison to the body length.

"Deep Brisket". The chest should be deep with the brisket reaching down to the elbow region.

"Chest not too broad". A chest that is too broad increases lateral displacement, causing incorrect movement.

"Ribs well sprung". Well sprung ribs are essential to allow for heart/lung room for a working dog. To see spring of rib you must look down on the dog from above. It should be seen from behind the shoulder blades, spreading out, then narrowing to the "waist".

The ribs must spring out well from the backbone and curve down gently to the brisket. Gordon Setters should not have a flat or slab sided ribcage.

"Back ribs deep". The back ribs are also important. If they are short the dog loses vital lung room. A Gordon lacking spring of rib and depth of body does not have the correct body type.

"Loins wide and slightly arched". The loins come between the last rib and the pelvis and should be wide and muscular as seen from above. It is an unsupported section of backbone and as with a suspension bridge, a slight arch increases its strength. This slight arch must not be confused with a roach or camel back, where the arch starts in the ribcage area. The arch should be only sufficient to provide structural strength.

On a dog with a correct length of body and a good-sized rib cage the coupling will be relatively short.

The most common faults with backs are those which dip and those which roach – a straight, level back is what is called for. Loaded shoulders and overly broad chests often go hand in hand and are not desirable. The brisket should extend to the elbows. A shallow chest can be camouflaged by long coat on the chest and so is not immediately evident unless one feels for it.

HINDQUARTERS
"From hip to hock long, broad and muscular, hock to heel short, strong, stifles well bent, straight from hock joint to ground. Pelvis tending to horizontal."
When assessing the hindquarters the stance of the dog is very important. The dog should be standing in a natural position with the rear pasterns (hocks) vertical when viewed both from the side and from behind.

The purpose for which the breed was developed should be remembered when assessing the hindquarters. The Gordon is required to display endurance when moving over uneven ground. As viewed from above the hindquarters should be broad and muscular.
"Pelvis tending to horizontal" is usually taken to mean that the croup should be level. However, a level croup is not desirable in a dog which is required to show drive behind or is expected to display endurance when moving over uneven ground. In a Gordon the croup should have a gentle slope flowing through from the "slightly arched loin". Therefore, in the Gordon, "pelvis tending to horizontal" should be taken to mean that the croup should not be steep but rather should be gently sloping to allow the dog to work properly.

Weak hindquarters often accompany an overly steep croup, as the steepness of the croup does not allow the formation of the broad, strong muscles needed for correct movement and endurance.
"From hip to hock, long, broad and muscular". The upper and lower thighs should be long and well muscled. The hindquarters should be broad and strong when examined both from the side and from the rear.
"Hock to heel, short and strong". A short strong rear pastern gives greater stability, than does a longer pastern.
"The stifles should be well bent". If hip to hock is long and the relative length of upper and lower thigh are approximately equal and the rear pasterns short and strong, the stifle should be well turned.
"Straight from hock joint to ground". The rear pasterns should be straight when viewed from the side. They should not be inclined either in or out when viewed from behind, when standing or moving.

The hindquarters should complement the forequarters and they should give the appearance of strength, stamina and drive.

The hindquarter angulation should not be over exaggerated.

FEET
"Oval, close knit, well arched toes, plenty of hair between. Well padded toes, deep heel cushions."
The Gordon was developed as a gundog required to work on uneven, heather-covered ground. Therefore, it is important that his feet should be sound with no sign of weakness. It is for this reason that the Standard calls for close-knit, well-arched, well-padded toes.

"Oval". The impression left by the foot should be oval rather than round. The centre toes are slightly longer than the outside toes.

"Close knit well arched toes". These help give grip. A Gordon should not have hare feet or be flat-footed.

"Plenty of hair between the toes" is thought to give the foot extra protection. However, the hair between the toes is often trimmed to prevent penetration of grass seed or the formation of mud balls.

"Well padded toes, deep heel cushions". (The heel cushion is more correctly called the communal pad.) The thick pads of the feet provide cushioning during movement.

The feet on a Gordon are of particular importance. A dog with flat feet and/or scattered toes will have great difficulty in doing the work required of him, so these faults should be penalised.

TAIL

"Straight or slightly scimitar, not reaching below hocks. Carried horizontally or below line of back. Thick at root, tapering to fine point. Feather or flag starting near root, long, straight, growing shorter to point".

"Straight or slightly scimitar". The tail should be straight or have a gentle curve, but shouldn't be hooked.

"Not reaching below the hocks". It should be of only moderate length. A long tail spoils the visual balance of the dog.

"Carried horizontally or below line of back". The tail is the final portion of the spine and should follow the flow of the spine.

"Thick at root, tapering to fine point". As the continuation of the spine a tail which is thick at the root indicates that the bones of the spine are of ample size.

The tail should be well feathered. The feathering is often trimmed to achieve the desired triangular shape.

MOVEMENT – GAIT

"Steady, free moving and true, plenty of drive".

The Gordon Setter has a characteristic, sound, balanced gait usually seen in an anatomically correct dog. The hindquarters are the driving force, requiring a combination of muscles in the pelvis and upper thighs, assisted by the lower thighs and short rear pasterns. The forequarters give the required forward reach and the front legs pull the ground in under the dog. When moving, the topline should be firm and level, giving a picture of free flowing effortless movement.

"Steady", firm, stable, temperate, industrious, reliable. Creates a picture of a purposeful, active individual, not rushing, but always working.

"Free moving", uninhibited, easy, elastic, strong, untiring movement. A free moving dog moves without restraint or restriction, which allows the dog to cover the ground well in an effortless manner.

"True" movement requires that the dog's front legs and rear legs move in straight lines following each other (not pacing). The dog will tend to centre track as the speed increases.

The gait should not be hampered by the twisting of joints, or inwards or outwards turned bone structure, all of which consume energy, causing the dog to tire quickly, and increase wear and tear in the joints.

"Plenty of drive". Driving hindquarters propel the dog forward. A short stepping or up-and-down movement is incorrect. A long strong thrusting movement is what is required. This drive is essential in a dog working all day over uneven terrain.

The Gordon Setter in the field has a questing gait, not moving in a straight line, but hunting back and forth across a field. The young Gordon requires understanding, as quite often they appear ungainly in the ring with their instinctive questing movement.

COAT

"On head, front of legs, tops of ears short and fine, moderate length, flat and free from curl or wave on all other parts of body. Feather on upper portion of ears long and silky, on backs of legs long, fine, flat and straight; fringes on belly may extend to chest and throat. As free as possible from curl or wave."

"On head, front of legs, tips of ears short and fine, moderate length, flat and free from curl or wave on all other parts of body." A slight wave in the coat is characteristic of many Gordon Setters and is generally considered acceptable, unless it is excessively wavy or curly.

"Feather on upper portion of ears long and silky, on backs of legs long, fine, flat and straight; fringes on belly may extend to chest and throat." Most adult Gordons will have fringing on the chest, but may have the throat fringe trimmed for showing. The fringing should be of only moderate length so as not to interfere with the dog's working ability.

"As free as possible from curl or wave" refers to the feathering and fringing. The texture of the coat should not be harsh or coarse nor so fine as to be wispy.

Many Gordons take 3-4 years to develop the heavier coat of the mature Gordon. Young dogs will therefore often not have much coat and should not be penalised for it.

COLOUR

"Deep shining coal black, without rustiness, with markings of chestnut red, i.e. lustrous tan."

Dead hair which has not been groomed out properly and which is dry in texture will give a rusty appearance. The tan markings should be a lustrous rich chestnut red, reminiscent of the colour of a ripe horse chestnut. Tan which is too pale and straw coloured should be penalised.

The Gordon Setter is a black and tan dog and the Standard is very detailed regarding the markings.

"Black pencilling on toes and black streak under jaw permissible. "Tan markings": two clear spots over eyes not over 2cm (3/4in) in diameter; on sides of muzzle (tan not reaching above base of nose), resembling a stripe around clearly defined end of muzzle from one side to other; on throat." The tan should come along each side of the muzzle and along the front of the muzzle under the nose and be clearly defined. It should not come above the base of the nose. The tan extends from under the jaw to about halfway down the length of the neck. The Standard does not mention that most Gordons have a "dewdrop" or a tan spot between the neck and eye which is partly concealed by the overlapping of the black hair.

The Gordon Setter is typified by a dignified, noble and intelligent expression.

Tan hair may also be found on the inside of the ears. Puppies very often have tan across the end of the nose which should later, with maturity, disappear. The tan markings of some Gordons darken or blacken as they grow older, most noticeably on the sides of the muzzle. **"Two large, clear spots on chest".** There should be two large clear and distinct spots on either side of the chest which are not joined. Sometimes the tan spots are obscured by the longer black hair of the chest coat.

"On inside hindlegs and inside thighs, showing down front of stifle and broadening out to outside of hindlegs from hock to toes; on forelegs, up to elbows behind, and to knees or a little above, in front; around vent. Very small white spot on chest permissible. No other colour permissible." White hair is sometimes found in the tan around the vent and is a minor fault. The black hair should be free of any tan hairs and likewise the tan should be free of black hair except as allowed in the Standard, the seriousness of the fault is relative to the degree of the mismarking. The clearer the colour and the markings the better.

However, it should be stated that an excellent specimen should not be discarded should the colour not be quite as required – other points must also be considered when making a judgement and these may be of more importance than colour.

SIZE
"Height: Dogs 66 cms (26 ins); Bitches 62 cms (24.1/2 ins)."
Although weight is not specified, the Gordon is a substantial dog for his height. His weight should come from muscle and bone, not excessive body fat.

Whilst extremes of height should be penalised, slight variations are not a major fault. Type, balance and soundness are more important.

NOTE: Male animals should have two apparently normal testicles fully descended into the scrotum.

FAULTS

"Any departure from the foregoing points should be considered a fault and the seriousness with which the fault should be regarded should be in exact proportion to its degree."

The present Standard does not specify any particular faults other than as stated above.

When assessing a Gordon it should be recognised that a fault that affects a dog's ability to do the work for which it was developed, or affects the health or well-being of the dog, should be viewed more seriously than faults which have only regard to the aesthetic qualities of the dog.

SUMMING UP

1. Colour – a black and tan dog.
2. Size – medium height with substance.
3. Total head – fairly long, skull deep, chiselled, noble.
4. Neck – long, arched.
5. Shoulders – long well laid back, flat. Upper arm well back under body. Together giving front vertical balance.
6. Chest – depth to elbow, with rib spring and ribbed well back.
7. Ribs – well sprung, back ribs deep.
8. Total body – of moderate length, not square or short, or too long.
9. Hindquarters – muscular, strong, with well bent stifles, short hocks. Pelvis tending horizontal.
10. Tail – short, carried out.

Chapter Four

COLOUR, COAT AND CONFORMATION

GENETIC INHERITANCE
Everything we see in our dogs has been inherited from their ancestors through their genetic structure. The gene pool is responsible for coat and colour. Genes also determine head and skull shape and have a great influence on conformation and bone structure. Therefore, in theory, if we took great care in keeping records, we should be able to foresee exactly what each mating would produce. However, it just is not that easy, especially where colour and coat texture are concerned.

COLOUR

In the early days, as the setter evolved from the setting spaniels, keepers concentrated on increasing their numbers and improving on their excellent working quality. Colours were mixed. It was later on, when the different setter breeds were being established by careful selection, that colour became important. It is easy to see the colour genes carried by the usual Gordon Setter. However, different ones do occur, from time to time, in liver and tan Gordons and all red Gordons, though they are born from black and tan parents.

According to the Breed standard for Gordon Setters, the colour which is acceptable is Black and Tan, black making the background colour and tan being found on the points of legs, feet and the skull. The other colours I have seen are liver and tan, red, black and tan with large splashes of white almost anywhere, and a Gordon who has a totally white background. The genetic formula for the black coat is -B-. There are, of course, other letters that give the shade of tan which can, in itself, be quite variable. It is the background colour which is all-important here. The lower-case letter -b- is used to represent any variation of brown, so B and b are really variations of the same colour. Therefore, the liver and tan Gordon is the product of a lower-case 'b' gene, which is also responsible for the red Gordon. This is only a brief explanation, as I am not a geneticist, and there are many publications on the subject which are well worth reading.

In the UK these recessive genes, the lower-case b gene, seem to run in cycles: that is to say, there might suddenly be quite a crop of, for example, liver and tan Gordons. Obviously, as breeders became aware of the sires that produced these colours, they quickly learned how to avoid it. I must emphasise, however, that colour differences cannot be blamed solely upon

Sh. Ch. Lourdace Graph Spae (Rossend Gaelic Storm – Sh. Ch. Lourdace Silica) showing the typical black and tan markings of a Gordon Setter.

The puppy in the foreground is black and tan, but the remaining two are liver and tan. Note the tan is located in exactly the same places, regardless of the background colour.

the sire, for the gene must be carried by both parents to get the liver and tan, or red colours, in the resulting litter.

AN EXPERIMENT IN INHERITANCE

I experienced this in one litter. I had suspected that it might occur, and so it proved when the litter was born. I had a dog, Sh. Ch. Gladstone of Lourdace, and a bitch, Sh. Ch. Lourdace Graph Spae. Their pedigrees ran rather close and from earlier conversations with older breeders, there was a likelihood that both my two might carry this recessive liver and tan gene. When they were mated, which was an accident and not at all intentional on my part, I made the decision to allow it to stand and not abort the pregnancy. If my suspicions were unfounded then, as both these two were excellent specimens of the breed, the litter could be super. Graph Spae had eight pups, four dogs and four bitches. One dog died and left a litter of seven, but three of the four bitches were liver and tan in colour; none of the males were affected. I retained the only black and tan bitch and mated her to a dog of similar pedigree who did not carry this gene; therefore all her pups were black and tan.

Daughters from this bitch have had varying effects on colour. One bitch, bred back to her grandfather who is a carrier of the recessive gene, produced a litter of six, of which one male was liver and tan. Another daughter has been mated to the same dog and produced a litter of seven, all black and tan. Of that original litter – my experiment in carrying the liver colour – one of the males, whilst he was black and tan in colour, had brown nostrils. He has been used at stud but, from looking at the pedigrees of the bitches, they do not carry this colour.

UNEXPECTED VARIATIONS

However, even from two parents where the recessive gene is active, not all the pups will inherit this tendency to the incorrect colours. I am sure that if it were possible to see genes, we would find that those pups who carried a heavy influence would show it. There would also be those who, although they are black and tan, would still carry it, but here the amount would vary from dog to dog. I know, by test matings that I have done, that some pups in the same litter do not carry the recessive gene at all, while siblings may do so. It is only by actually mating two Gordons together that you can safely establish whether there is an incidence of recessive colour.

I have had no personal experience of red Gordons. There is one breeder in the UK who used to get quite a lot of pups who were red, but this does not occur any more in her present stock. A breeder in New Zealand has just had a litter of Gordons and three of these were 'blue' in colour. I have not seen photos of them yet but, talking on the telephone about them, I gather that they are the same colour as the 'Isabella' or fawn Dobermann. These dogs are born a bluey shade which fades to fawn as they grow. This is the first time I have heard of this particular colouring in Gordon setters. As far as I know it does not exist in the UK.

Looking back, before my time in Gordons, and asking a few questions, I find that liver and tan Gordons were quite common in the 1960s. I have documentation of one being registered

Field Trial Champion Freebirch Vincent: A law unto himself, with a white coat which has black and tan markings.

as liver and tan and another one registered as being brown. As I understand it, both were bred from. After this, the British Gordon Setter Club requested that the Kennel Club should not allow dogs with this colouring to be registered, but at the present time they are being accepted.

There is one Gordon in the UK, however, which shows that genes are not responsible for everything. Field Trial Champion Freebirch Vincent was registered by the breeder as being black, tan and white! In fact he is a dog with a white background, with some black patching and a few tan marks on his body. In the UK, the KC has no means of making a check on the actual markings of any dog, or the precise placement of colour, so the registration went through. This dog is the subject of much questioning, even though he is a Field Trial Champion. His owner, Bob Truman, has consented to Dr. Willis, an expert in canine genetics, looking into the matter, as even Bob does not believe that there has not been a mishap here. There were three whelps in the litter who were this colour, the remainder being black and tans.

The fact is that there are many genes carried by Gordon Setters but the B and b genes are dominant. When a dog arrives with a totally different background colour, then questions will be asked. As for the rest, if breeders were honest and kept a record in which to register peculiarities of any kind, then working out how to avoid a problem would be extremely easy.

The tan colour on the Gordon is affected by genetic make-up in the same way, but those breeders who have managed to establish a rich tan seldom seem to lose it. There are some lines where the tan is the colour of straw and not desirable, but this can be changed by careful breeding and careful selection.

COAT

THE CASE FOR A LONG COAT
The coat of a Gordon Setter can be seen around the world in many different types. Quite often, each owner is convinced that their dog is correct and everyone else is wrong. This is particularly true of the owners of Gordons with very little coat at all. Beauty, as we all know, is in the eye of the beholder, but I would not really believe anyone who shows Gordons if they told me they disliked the long, profuse coat carried by so many winners in the ring.

It can be seen that those dogs who support a wealth of long silky hair win over those who do not. I have spoken to breeders who cannot produce coat and have listened to their reasons as to why they prefer that type. Usually they claim that too much coat is incorrect. Yet, when they manage to produce coat, we do not hear them complain!

Personally, I believe that although type, in any breed, starts with the head of the animal, the next important consideration is the coat. Certainly the field dog, who may have to cover ground of sharp heather, will need some protection for head, neck, forechest and shoulders while pushing into thick undergrowth, following the scent to find quarry. A heavy coat is essential, otherwise the Gordon will not last a season without injury. I am sure that the long tresses we see on the show dog would simply be pulled out on the gorse and brambles. But that is exactly the point. At least it is there to be pulled out. It cannot be any joy for a dog who is poorly coated to work in dense cover.

Sh. Ch. Dudmoor Mylton of Lourdace: A long, profuse coat is highly valued in the show ring – but this does not have to be at odds with the rugged nature of the breed. This dog has had a tremendous influence on the breed, winning the national award of Top Sire on eight occasions.

Bert and Mary Dyde.

A Gordon Setter is, or should be, the most rugged of the setters. This ruggedness will appear on the skull as if sculptured, or as we say, a head with much work in it. While I do not believe that any Gordon should have a curly coat, one with slight wave does add to the character of the dog. It is also very true that those with no wave never appear to grow any great length in their coat and never appear to have the great density required to keep the weather out. A Gordon whose coat is on the short side, with no undercoat, will not do well in rain and poor weather conditions and will not thrive in the hands of someone who rough shoots, staying out for most of the day, in all kinds of weather.

There is also the coat which is fine and likened to wool. This may not be quite desirable in a Gordon kept as a pet, as it will need too much grooming if the hair is not to become matted. Much as I love my pet owners, and much as they love their Gordons, they do often unintentionally neglect their Gordons' coats, so a happy medium is required to keep everyone content.

As for myself, I adore the profuse coat. I have had Gordons who did not carry enough coat for me. One bitch just missed her title because of her lack of coat. True, there was no work to be done on her, but I felt as if I had missed out on show preparation if I didn't have to use my finger and thumb, and do some hair removing, before the event. I even felt quite cheated.

Coat is bred in and, while there are many preparations to be bought to enhance the coat if the genes have not provided sufficient quality, nothing will make a coat grow longer. It also reflects the dog's health and condition. A coat lacking lustre is a sign that the dog is not in tiptop condition, or may be lacking a vital dietary requirement.

CONFORMATION

FOREQUARTERS

Correct shoulder angulation is essential if the Gordon Setter is to move with the easy, balanced, tireless gait, which is necessary for the working dog. To be correct, the length of the shoulder blade (scapula) must be equal to the length of the upper arm (humerus). It is common to see many Gordon Setters with a shorter upper arm compared to the shoulde blade, giving rise to a stance similar to that of a rocking horse. However, equal lengths of these two bones does not neccessarily mean that the shoulder is correctly laid back.

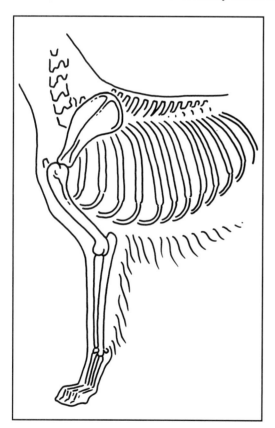
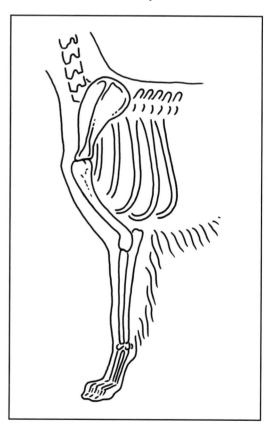

CORRECT SHOULDERS: This enlargement of forehand construction illustrates how the large structure copes with weight-bearing, and gives the balance which every judge is searching for.

UPRIGHT SHOULDERS: This fault almost always leads to a rough juncture of the neck, shoulder and back. The steep angle of the neck is apparent, compared with the correct construction.

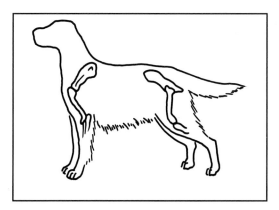

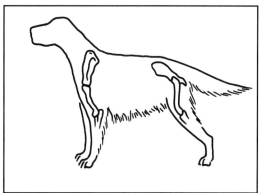

The good angulation shown here will allow this dog to move with a good length of stride, covering a great deal of ground quite effortlessly.

A dog with these shoulders is quite likely to move with a lowered head carriage on the forehand, and with very little drive from the rear quarters, the forehand doing most of the work. Notice that poor angulation of the shoulders runs hand in hand with poor angulation of the rear assembly. Seldom is one end good and the other poor; dogs nearly always carry similar angulation both fore and aft.

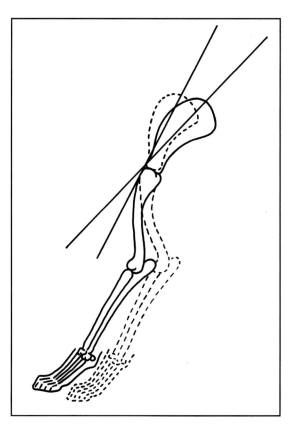

The length and lift of stride is affected by shoulder blade angulation.

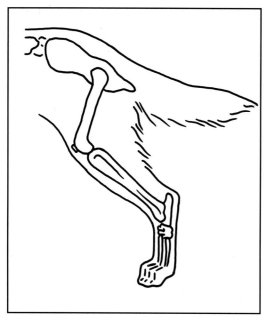

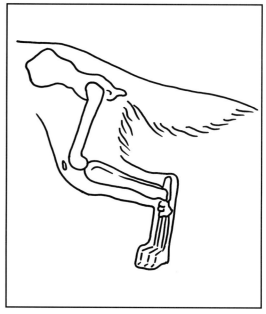

This portrays correct angulation of the rear assembly. It would prove to be extremely useful to the working dog, and it would be a pleasure to watch this type of specimen moving.

This dog has an over-angulated stifle. Fortunately, it is rarely seen in Gordon Setters. This dog would find galloping extremely difficult and would tire easily.

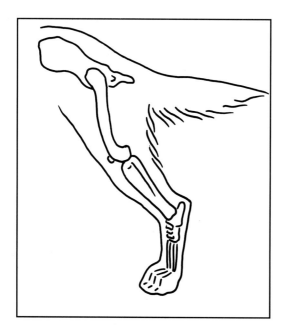

This rear shows too little angulation, making for a steep croup which in turn leads to a shorter stride. In order to increase speed, this dog would quicken his step rather than lengthen his stride.

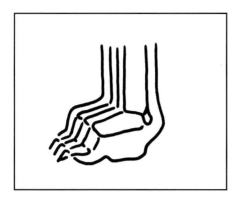

This shows how the bones should be positioned to give well arched toes and good pasterns. Note the substantial heel cushion, well let down on to the ground.

HINDQUARTERS

Although much has been written about the shoulders and their effect upon balance and movement in the Gordon, we must also consider the hindquarters which are of equal if not more importance than the forehand. All drive must come from behind in any animal. This enables effortless movement for lengthy periods, but it can only occur if the structure is correct.

Everyone is surely familiar with mathematics and the power of levers. It is on a similar principle that the dog's hind angulation gives rise to a bone structure which really is a series of levers all driving each other forward, lifting and causing a lengthening of the stride. Good rear angulation allows the dog to raise the forehand effortlessly, and as a working Gordon it is necessary to have the head high to pick up body scent. The proportions of the long bones in the hind leg (that is, the femur and tibia and fibula) must be correct to allow true movement. The angulation of both the forehand (shoulders) and rear assembly are almost always equal to each other; therefore a dog with poor shoulder assembly is not liable to be any better in the construction of his rear. It is good breeding and an understanding of dominant genes that breed this good conformation.

A typical British Gordon Setter head which is deep rather than broad. The muzzle should be long with almost parallel lines. It should not be pointed or snipey.

HEAD SHAPES

The shape of the head and skull is influenced by inherited genes. Only occasionally does this system fall foul and congenital faults arise.

A typical Australian head. Note the light eyes, and the rounded appearance of the muzzle.

THE BITE

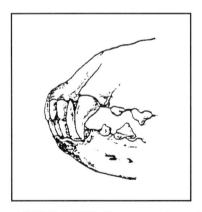

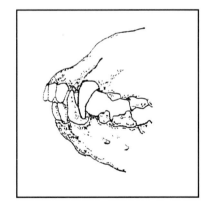

ABOVE LEFT: Correct: scissor bite.

ABOVE RIGHT: The construction of the mouth shown above is very common in a young Gordon. They are very often penalised and owners told by some judges and those who officiate at training and ring handling sessions, that this is incorrect. In fact this just isn't true. I would want to see a mouth with the dentition in an indentical state, until my youngster was at least nine or ten months of age. Should the bite be any tighter at a younger age, it would be highly likely to become, at best, level and at worst, completely undershot.

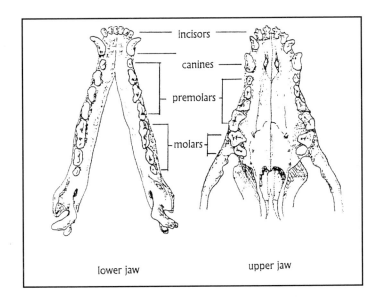

**CORRECT
DENTITION**

*Dentition layout of
top and bottom jaws
in a Gordon Setter.*

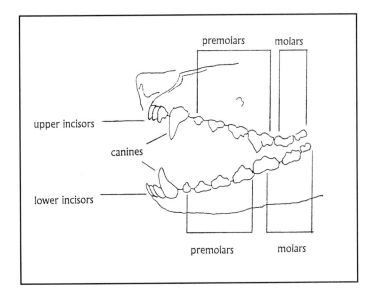

*The correct layout of
teeth enables efficient
grinding of food.*

DENTITION

The Gordon Setter should have strong jaws, and a perfect, complete scissor bite with the upper teeth closely overlapiing the lower teeth and set square to the jaws. Complete dentition is preferable.

Chapter Five

CHOOSING A PUPPY

DECIDING YOUR INTENTIONS

The first consideration, when buying a Gordon puppy, must be a decision as to what this puppy is intended to do. Several differences can be noticed, even in puppies still in the nest, and future plans will influence the initial choice. Do you want your Gordon to work, either as a rough shooting dog or as a serious field trialler? Do you wish to show and will that showing become serious, as in Championship Shows, or just for fun, such as the show held in the village each year? Or, maybe, this pup is to be a pet, involved with children and a home lifestyle, or perhaps be a companion to adults where there are no children? Each criterion leads to a different choice of pup and, in some cases, a different type of breeder.

FIELD TRIALS

Anyone with serious intentions of keen, hard field trialling should approach a Gordoner successful in that particular skill. It is rather sad that any breed is allowed to split into a 'them' and 'us' situation, but I'm afraid that this does exist. The successful field trial man will have his finger firmly on the pulse and will be breeding from winning stock that have proved to be keen hunters, with exceptional ability to scent game birds, wherever they are and whatever the weather conditions. Sometimes, within such a kennel, the breed standard is ignored, and replaced by an overwhelming desire to win, and there is no doubt that the pups produced will fit the bill for anyone wishing to own such a keen dog.

THE DOMESTIC PET

This same animal, however, may not ever fit into your particular home as a pet. Natural instincts would always be taking over and that leisurely morning stroll could well become a frenzied search for game by a hunting Gordon who has become deaf to the call of the owner.

THE SHOW RING

Neither would a dog from this type of stock become suitable for the serious exhibitor, as many of them, bred for their nose only, have missing teeth, incorrect bites and a variety of coats, sizes and colours.

CHOOSING A BREEDER

Bearing all this information in mind, a purchaser must first of all ascertain which breeders to approach in the quest to obtain a Gordon. Here the Kennel Club will play a large part, as it will furnish enquirers with a list of breeders and information about whether they breed for work, show or play.

  Having made a decision about the type of Gordon required, you should contact the breeder and ask as many questions as possible. Avoid, at all costs, the puppy farmer, and make sure you arrive at the door of a knowledgeable, caring breeder. Do ask to see the puppies with their mother. This will allow you to judge whether her temperament is desirable. Always visit on more than one occasion, if you possibly can, as puppies do change a little as they grow. It would also be seriously advisable to order your puppy before it is born, allowing time for you to learn and prepare for this new arrival.

SORTING PUPPIES ON A TABLE

The best method of assessing conformation is to stand the puppy on a table.

Go through the litter one by one comparing individual attributes.

Evaluating an eight-week-old puppy's head shape.

MAKING YOUR CHOICE

When you finally visit, to choose your precious bundle, always allow plenty of time to sit and observe, before making your decision. If you wish to show, then your eye should be on conformation as well as temperament. It is desirable to have a pup that is something of an extrovert. This will prove to be an asset in the eyes of judges, because the puppy is sure to acquire a certain amount of ring presence and probably grow up to become a great 'show off'.

Don't choose this puppy if you want a pet, as you may be driven to distraction with lively activities that seem never to pall. To take home the perfect pet, you need the pup who is rather laid back, not over-eager to charge about all over the place and tending towards a much calmer nature. However, do not confuse this pup with the nervous and shy one, for this type often become so reticent as to resent and fear others and may, in time, become so frightened that the automatic response is to bite at any perceived threat.

It must also be calculated that this dog may be with you for twelve or more years, the probable life-span, so the correct choice is very important. You may be really lucky and have the puppy choose you – then everything will be just right.

APPRECIATING DIFFERENCES

Reading the Breed Standard for the Gordon Setter, without photos, pictures and live models with which to make comparisons, sets a difficult task in appreciating the differences that

OVERALL CONSTRUCTION

At eight weeks old these litter brothers show that difference in construction is visible at a very early age. The discerning breeeder seeking to retain the best show prospect would retain the puppy pictured left. His litter brother is a reasonable specimen, but he does not have the quality that is already apparent in his sibling.

Two bitches pictured from the same litter as the two male puppies. In this case, the puppy with the best construction is pictured on the right.

SHOULDER ANGULATION

This puppy excels in shoulder angulation, with good proportions of upper arm and shoulder blade. He has plenty of forechest, which is of good depth, and neat elbows. He has a good hind-end and stifle, and he also has correct ear-set.

This puppy does not have such good shoulder construction. The upper arm is rather steep, although the shoulder is well-laid. The croup is steeper, spoiling the topline.

This puppy is the poorest of the three in shoulder construction. Note the protruding elbow and shorter coupling.

BODY PROPORTIONS

This puppy lacks depth and is too long in the body. He may grow up to be like the adult pictured below, who has the same problems.

Dogs built like this very seldom have the ability to lengthen their stride at the trot. However, a novice judge could assume the dog was moving well: as the body is so long the rear assembly readily follows the front, and the joints appear quite straight. In fact, it is the faulty length in the loin which gives this appearance. The loin is weak by virtue of the extra length, and would prove tiring to a dog expected to work all day.

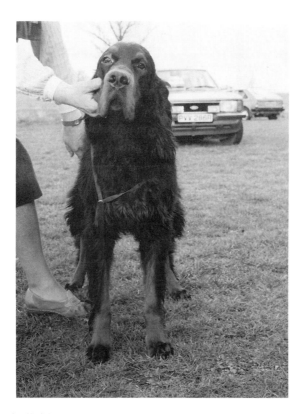

This six-month-old male shows a correct, straight front. Notice how the descent of the shoulder continues straight down to the front legs. Bone is carried down to the feet, with no deviations, either inward or outward, of any joint.

exist between individual Gordons. Although some such differences are of detriment to the animal, there are some which are not, and here it is quite true to say, once again, that "Beauty is in the eye of the beholder". In these circumstances two very well-versed judges may disagree without making any mistakes.

Many of the pups seen in our illustrations will make the reader aware of differences, even between young ones who are litter mates. Although most of the photos are side views, take an interest in all angles, both fore and aft. Whatever attributes the pups have when they are young, will still be with them as adults and, in some cases, may have improved. The usual method for sorting out a litter is to place one of the pups on a table and evaluate it, then place another one to compare the two, and so on through the litter. Whichever one is still on the table, when the whole litter has been examined, is the best of the litter. Hopefully, the litter is of top quality and each new owner is hoping that their chosen one will be the world beater!

Chapter Six

BREEDING AND THE
CHOICE OF STUD DOG

Every bitch owner has, at some time, to make decisions about breeding. If the bitch was purchased with the intention of breeding from her, then it is a question of when and with whom. If the bitch is a pet, the owner, at some time, may decide to breed her in order to keep one of the puppies to have as a companion now and a replacement later.

MAKING IMPORTANT CHECKS

It is not a decision to be taken lightly, as not all bitches should be bred from, for a variety of reasons. These can include health, construction and age. There are checks which can, and must, be done to establish the existence, or the absence, of some conditions.

 It is most important is to examine the hips and determine whether or not there is any hip dysplasia and, if there is, just how bad it is. In the UK there is a hip scoring scheme, monitored by Dr Malcolm B. Willis, lecturer on genetics at Newcastle University, who devised it and keeps records of all scores. In Europe a similar scheme is also in operation, supervised, in the case of Gordons, by the Setter and Pointer Clubs. In America, too, there is a hip X-raying scheme in being. They may appear to differ in their recording and scoring but, basically, all these methods send the same messages.

 If the would-be breeder is satisfied about the dog's hips, then a general health check should be made by the vet. *As a stud dog owner, I would not accept just any bitch.* I would need to know that she was 'clean', which means that she is not carrying any infection in her vagina that may be passed to my dog. No bitch should be bred from until she is either two years old or on her third season, unless there is a veterinary reason to breed earlier.

CHOOSING THE SIRE

Now we come to the choice of the sire for this litter. This is not something to take lightly and there are many aspects that should receive careful consideration. Firstly, this animal must have something that you find easy on the eye, or perhaps I should say he must be a dog you like. As there is a Breed Standard, do adhere to it. If you do, hopefully, the sire will meet the Standard and be a good specimen of the breed.

 Then take a look at the dog's pedigree. My reason for this is that I find that more quality is to be found in litters that are line-bred. That is to say, there are some animals, amongst their antecedents, that are common to both the dog and the bitch. Inbreeding is also useful, but

Northinch Briar of Keepersgate (Sh. Ch. Lourdace Mink – Northinch Black Rose): Top Stud Dog in 1992 and 1993, and a highly influential sire for the Lourdace kennel.

Bert and Mary Dyde.

should be left to experts, with vast historical knowledge of the breed from which to draw information. If there are no common factors in either pedigree, then this is called 'outcrossing'. I have tried this, for a variety of reasons, but have yet to be satisfied with what was produced. Outcrossing often produces giants, in my experience. It does widen the gene pool but the litters tend to be larger, plainer and very ordinary, with nothing truly outstanding. However, a good specimen can result and should then be retained, if only to breed back into the established line of the breeder.

Then one needs to assess the dog's virtues and ask oneself the following questions: 'What does this dog have that I want?' and 'What does this dog have that I don't want?' Having reached some conclusion about this, take a look at the bitch and ask the same two questions. Take stock, and decide where the bitch could be improved, or where this male may do some harm and damage an already established, sound structure.

After this exercise has been completed, then take a look at what this dog has already produced, in other words, his progeny. One does need, however, to view his progeny in conjunction with the bitch who was mated to him. Here one needs to decide whether the sire is dominant, or whether the progeny lean heavily in looks to their mother. The question to ask is: 'Does this male reproduce himself, or are all the whelps younger versions of their

Am. Ch. Heavenly Current Choice with four of his Champion offpring. This outstanding sire has more than ninety American Champions to his name. Owned by Loree Ragano of the Heavenly kennel.

mother?' Try to see as many of his stock as you can. It will not be worthwhile using him to improve what you already have in your bitch, unless he can pass these qualities on.

A POINT TO AVOID

Certainly there is one thing not to do, and that is automatically to use the male who is currently winning in the show ring. He may have a heavy and profuse coat and be such a show-off that he catches the judge's eye enough times to finish top of his breed at the end of the year. But, by the same token, he may be hiding many structural faults underneath all that coat and, in this case, it is probably his personality that wins through. If you use the question-and-answer system, then apply it to the top winning male of the day. If your conclusion is the correct one, then use him by all means. One of the best ways of trying to improve is to find a male that really catches your eye, and, if he is line bred to your bitch, then it may be to your advantage to use the sire that produced this animal.

THE RESPONSIBILITY OF BREEDING

Always remember that we are only the caretakers of this breed and, when we are gone, it is hoped that we have left it in better order than we found it and, certainly, we must not have changed it, or left it the poorer for our efforts.

When you are new to the breed, it is difficult to acquire sufficient knowledge even of the animals named in the pedigree of your own setter. So it is wise to talk over any breeding plans with someone who has a wider knowledge and whose advice is worth having. Certainly one should not take the first offer without some thought. People who have been in the breed longer will have some idea of faults carried by the ancestors of your bitch. They will also know where the influences are liable to come from. So do not just seek advice from one person, but from many, and then peruse what you have learned.

PREPARATIONS FOR MATING

Before the mating takes place, there are one or two things to remember and take care of. For instance, make sure all inoculations are up to date, including and especially those for Parvovirus. One always hopes that no one will ever breed from a bitch that is not in perfect health, as this would lead to puppies of poor qualities, should they survive. If in doubt, take the bitch along to the vet for a general health check.

Food is of great importance and one hopes that all Gordons, whether they are to be bred from or not, will be fed on a good-quality and well-balanced diet. If one of the complete foods is being used, then all the requirements for good health will be already present and there is no need to provide any supplements. Too many additives will have just as bad an effect as if none were being fed at all. I am not a great believer in the very high protein foods that are so readily available and I make twenty per cent protein my limit.

TIMING AND SCHEMING

Although the normal gestation period is sixty-three days, each bitch will be slightly different. This also applies to the mating of bitches. There are three stages of the 'season', or 'heat' as it is sometimes called. The first stage is the swelling of the vulva, the second is the bleeding, or spotting, stage and the third is known as the period of ovulation.

This is the only time the bitch will allow herself to be mated. A mating at any other time will not lead to pregnancy.

Bitches, in the wild, choose their mate some six weeks before they even come into season, and this principle still applies to the domesticated animal. Therefore this can lead to problems when a bitch lives with a male, but one who is not the owner's choice of stud! I keep three stud dogs, and four bitches, all living together in harmony, but I have experienced problems when I need to mate one of the bitches, if the male is not her choice. Accordingly, when my bitches come into season, I send them away to kennels so as not to aggravate the males. If I want to mate one of my bitches to one of my males, I send the other males to live elsewhere until I have managed the mating: if I want to use one of my younger males, this absence prevents the top stud from making his presence felt by dominating the younger male into a refusal to mate.

The correct time for mating is when ovulation occurs; any other time would be unproductive. Each bitch will have her own time for ovulation and no two bitches are the same. Some even appear to ovulate when still showing bright coloured spots.

Ovulation occurs when the bleeding has stopped or, at least, lost most of the colour and, at this time, the vulva will have started to shrink back, almost to normal size. My advice, to the owners of bitches who are mating their Gordons for the first time, is to wait until the bleeding stops, check by swabbing with a tissue, and then bring the bitch two days later. Often owners worry that they may miss the right time and they arrive too early. The bitch is then unwilling and can surprise her owners by her natural response to an unwanted suitor, which is to use her teeth.

I would far rather get a mating both animals are agreeable to than try to force the issue, which invariably spoils the bitch for another time and can result in small litters or none at all. It is tantamount to rape, and I will have no part in that.

MATING

All I ask is that the visiting bitch wears a collar. I am not a party to muzzles or any other form of restraint for the bitch. I prefer that, once the visiting bitch is in a safe place, with all doors closed and no escape route, then the stud dog is introduced. At this time neither are restrained and there is time for each to become accustomed to the other. This period may last from fifteen to thirty minutes. I have never witnessed any aggression that my males could not simply avoid, by skipping out of the way, without sustaining any damage to themselves. The vibes that the two canines emit, one to the other, are only known to themselves. We humans are not privileged to be able to translate. The male will be fully aware of just how dangerous, or otherwise, this strange bitch is and he does not need us to interfere by holding or restraining in any way. If the time has been calculated successfully, there will be a natural mating – during which I hold the bitch's collar to prevent her sitting down or dragging my stud dog all over the place, as, once there is a tie, the male cannot be freed.

The sperm from the male is ejaculated in two or more doses. The first lot, known as premate, is quite often not fertile as it has been held within the testicles for some time, ever since the dog was last used in fact. So it is important for the tie to last as long as is required for the next ejaculation of fresh and fertile sperm. The dogs will not come apart until the bitch lets go. This is involuntary on her part. She has no knowledge that it is she who is responsible for this sometimes uncomfortable posture. She has a muscle just inside the vulva, which responds to the pressure from the enlarged penis and prevents it being withdrawn. It can sometimes be observed that there are muscular spasms occurring both from the bitch and the dog. It is not known whether this movement keeps the dog's penis enlarged for a greater length of time, or whether it is an attempt to bring the whole procedure to an end.

At the time of establishing the 'tie' the male, of his own volition turns, lifts one hind leg completely over the bitch so that they are standing back to back. Often people, in conversation, refer to a 'good' mating. By this they mean that there was a 'tie' and this was spread over some twenty to thirty minutes.

Some stud dog owners prefer the dog to remain mounted on top of the bitch. I have no idea what their reasoning is, but I would not want my bitch to carry the weight of a heavy male for that amount of time. I have a male who is only of medium height and some visiting bitches are taller than him. Sometimes he elects not to turn but to drop down and remain standing at the side of the bitch. Turning, or standing back to back, causes no injury to the male, as his scrotum is designed to revolve through one hundred and eighty degrees; so there is no need for concern.

UNDERSTANDING POSSIBLE PROBLEMS

It is not advisable to mate two maidens together for their first experience. A young male may well be put off by an inexperienced bitch, who could turn quite nasty at the point of entry and mete out severe punishment that an older and more experienced stud would simply ignore, and vice versa. Or the maiden male may become so excited at the sex scent he is picking up that he is too anxious and appears to be getting it all wrong, ejaculating before he has even entered. Don't worry, he will get it right in his own time and will not miss your bitch – the ovulation will last two to three days before a bitch finds the male's advances distasteful.

Whatever happens, don't interfere. On one occasion, I was called to assist with a mating. It was the owners of the bitch who pleaded for help. They told me that their bitch was standing with her tail round and inviting the dog, who was mounting her and then getting down. As both of these Gordons were experienced animals, I puzzled over their difficulties all the way to the home in question. Well, yes, the bitch was ready, and the dog seemed eager, so I watched, waiting to work out where the difficulty lay. This soon became apparent for, as the dog offered to mount the bitch, so her owner, who was holding the bitch's collar, leaned forward and, with considerable force, grabbed the dog and hauled him aboard. This was nothing more than over-handling of the male. As soon as I pointed this out and she left him alone, there was a good mating within minutes.

One needs to understand why the mating should take place at the optimum time. The bitch places her tail to one side which means that she has slightly hollowed her back which, in turn, causes the vulva to slightly protrude, almost teasing the male. This ensures that entry will be easy as, when the male mounts the bitch, his two front feet meet together in the area of the vulva and pushes it more towards his penis, ensuring correct direction and easy entry. None of this happens in cases of rape or at any other time during the season. So one can see that any outside interference, such as trying to aim the dog's penis or struggling to hold a bitch to get an unwilling mating, just hinders the whole process and leads to frustration all round. Leave nature to its own devices and it will work well.

There are several reasons why a tie does not take place. One is that the male is so dysplastic that he cannot round his back to get close enough to penetrate. Another is that the bitch's vulva is still swollen and not yet ready to hold on to the dog's penis.

Sometimes the bitch has an infection and, although there is a mating and a tie, there are no whelps. So please be sensible: seek advice from either your vet or another knowledgeable and responsible breeder. If one of my younger males is to be used for the first time, difficulties can arise because here at home he is the underdog, dominated by the top stud whose influence may lead the younger one into not performing. In this case, providing the owner of the bitch is willing, and does not own a male, I would certainly suggest taking the stud to the bitch's home. Some people prefer their bitch to be mated twice, but, if the correct day has been calculated, I am of the opinion that one good mating is sufficient.

FEEDING DURING PREGNANCY

When your bitch is known to be pregnant, then a slight rise in the protein level of her food is necessary, to allow sufficient nutrition for both mother-to-be and the unborn whelps.

It is not necessary to feed the pregnant bitch any extra food until after she has whelped. She may well appear to be ravenous and, so often, one hears owners saying how hungry their bitch is, and that they must increase the food so as to allow the bitch enough to feed the unborn litter as well as herself. This is totally unnecessary, and can lead to problems after whelping, such as mastitis. The process of increasing food and the number of feeds per day is known as 'steaming up', and any animal, not only canines, will go down with mastitis, or milk fever, as a result. The correct way of ensuring that the bitch has sufficient for her needs is to increase the protein content of her food in the sixth week of pregnancy. I never use a food that is higher than twenty-seven per cent at this stage.

ALLOWING FOR NATURAL INSTINCTS

The pregnant bitch's behaviour is often instinctive, and this is the reason for her increase in appetite. In the wild she would have to increase her body fat during pregnancy as, until her whelps were about one week old, she would be unable to leave them to hunt for food. She would live on her own reserves and the after-births until she felt able to forage for her meals. I often say to brood bitches "Now, now, I am going to feed you sufficiently after your puppies are born!"

Problems can arise at whelping which are the result of old instincts aroused by pregnancy. When I had horses, the yard consisted of twelve looseboxes, which were arranged on two sides of the yard. The third side was completed by a large brick barn in which hay was stored. On the fourth side was a tall thorn hedge, which had been allowed to grow both for shelter from the biting east wind and to make a fairly solid side to my paddock, which was used for breaking and schooling young horses. I had, at this time, a couple of dogs: one was an over-the-standard golden retriever and the other a crossbred collie that had been dumped on our doorstep one cold Christmas morning. This was in 1958, when very little was known about spaying, so every time the collie came into season, I fastened her into one of the empty looseboxes. It seems that occasionally, when I was away from the yard, she would manage to get out, but most of the time she was put back before I returned and I had no knowledge of her escape.

Eventually it became very obvious that she was definitely in whelp. I was very fond of her and took great care to feed her properly and prepare somewhere for her to have her puppies. Time went on and one day I realised that she had not been around to be fed. This went on for some five to six days and, when she did finally appear in the yard, I knew that she had disappeared to have her puppies. I fed her and decided to keep my eye on her so as to discover the whereabouts of the new arrivals but, after feeding, she settled down in the yard to snooze. I got on with my work with one eye on my bitch.

Suddenly, I realised that she had gone! I had not even seen in which direction she had disappeared, but I guessed that it would be into one of the fields. I tried searching and calling her name, Ginger, but to no avail. She kept up this pattern of behaviour for approximately four weeks and then, one day, she entered the yard from the direction of the fields and, quite obviously, wished to be seen. I welcomed her and she turned away, leading me towards the field. I followed, which seemed to please her, for she preceded me with a wagging tail and at a gentle pace. Ginger led me to where a fallen tree had laid its trunk across a wide ditch. The old timber was partly covered with long grasses that grew from each side. Down she went, into the dry bottom of the ditch. I saw that there was a hole beneath the trunk, in the wall of earth, and here were three young pups, precariously balanced at its edge. This bitch had wanted me to find them, as now they required more than just milk to sustain them. Although a domesticated dog, some of her natural instincts were still quite strong, but she also valued her human companions, especially where food was concerned.

Ginger repeated this process on two more occasions, each time selecting a new place to use for her babes. I never found any of them until she wanted me to. This need to whelp and stay in a private place, as it were, can be witnessed when whelping takes place within our homes or in our kennels. Bitches often prefer to be in the dark and, at times, attempt to get into the most impossible places. Once I was whelping one of mine in a bedroom and, when I was not about after the birth, she spent half her time trying to dig underneath my divan bed and ruined a carpet in the process. I solved this problem by covering half of the top of the whelping box with strong thick card which had been wrapped around my new cooker that had just been delivered. I fastened the back and sides of the box with some staples, making it firm so that it could not be dislodged. The bitch could now choose to lie in the shade or under the lamp. She settled for this and stopped all her scratching and digging. With her subsequent litters, I set off with the arrangement already in place at the onset of labour and experienced no more trouble.

One must try to take advantage of these dormant instincts, as they are often very strong. We can use them to help make the bitch better satisfied. Trying to ignore them can lead to problems. Although the dog has been domesticated since history was first recorded, some things lie much deeper than we are prepared to admit.

Chapter Seven

PREGNANCY AND WHELPING

THE IMPORTANCE OF EXERCISE
Having mated your bitch, and understood the requirements for her diet, some consideration must be given to her exercise. The fitter she is, the easier her time will be when the puppies are born. Therefore her exercise should remain the same, although it is reasonable to expect her to slow down and travel at a steadier pace as she increases in weight.

GUARDING AGAINST INFECTIONS
The ten-day period after the mating has taken place is all-important, because if there is any rise in the bitch's temperature due to infection, no matter how mild, this will prevent fertilisation of the ovum or eggs. I mention this because I had a bitch who, persistently, had tonsilitis after every season and, in my ignorance, I wasted a lot of time not getting puppies because I did not understand the signficance of the rise in temperature Eventually she was prescribed a mild antibiotic throughout her season, which warded off any infection she may have picked up, and I was pleased when she did produce.

THE DANGERS OF GOING OVER TIME
Although most bitches have a gestation period of sixty-three days, this can be cut short, or lengthened, for the following reasons: if the litter is large and heavy, the puppies will be born when there is no more room inside the womb, and, if the litter is small, or the whelps are very tiny, the bitch may go on longer. I personally do not like my bitches to go over their time, especially if I have had a scan taken and I know that there are only two, or even three puppies. The longer they stay inside the womb the bigger they grow, which makes for difficulties, especially if it is a first litter for a maiden bitch.

On several occasions, I have had a Gordon with a small number of puppies, and they have been born on time. Those that were going over time I took to the vet, and sometimes the advice was that the puppies were all right and they would arrive when they were ready! Well, in these cases they did come when they were ready – but they were dead. If that ever happens to me now, and my bitch is going over time, my vet knows that I am meticulous in my care for my brood bitches, and he will perform a caesarian. But I have to say that these whelps do not always survive. This is because there is already a problem, which is why they were late in the first place.

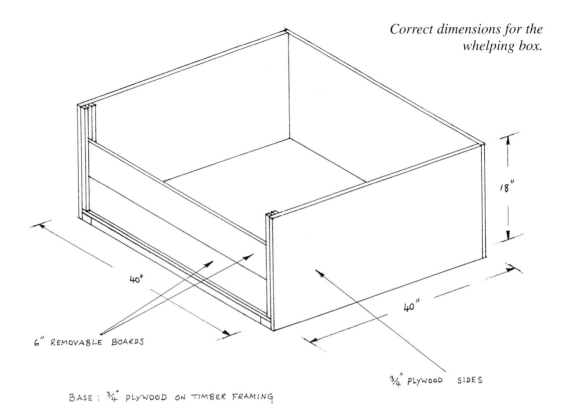

Correct dimensions for the whelping box.

18"

40"

40"

6" REMOVABLE BOARDS

3/4" PLYWOOD SIDES

BASE : 3/4" PLYWOOD ON TIMBER FRAMING

THE WHELPING BOX

There are several things every breeder must gather together before the whelping date draws near. The first thing you need to acquire is a whelping box. This is very necessary and do not imagine for one moment that you can make do without it. That attitude will cost you some, if not all, of your puppies. My box is forty inches square. It has three sides that are eighteen inches high and one side, which I refer to as the front, twelve inches high. This last side, or front, slides in between two runners and so it may be removed, if required, and also be added to in height.

The reasons for the measurements are as follows: the floor space is big enough to allow any Gordon Setter bitch to lie on her side at full stretch in comfort. The height of the eighteen-inch sides is to prevent draughts and, later, to prevent puppies climbing out. The shorter front allows the bitch, in the early days, to step in and out, eliminating the need to jump and run the risk of injury to the young. Neither will she drag her udder over the hard wooden sides – by now it will be very heavy with the milk she must produce for the survival of the oncoming litter – it could cause bruising, which may lead to mastitis. The box is easily made and, when completed, should sit well-fastened on to two skids, allowing a good airflow underneath and not allowing condensation to form.

Too much space does not improve the situation for the bitch herself. It may prove to be draughty with too much air circulating around, which can worry her and leave her far too restless to get on with the job in hand. This can have the effect of her trying to put off the actual birth, dropping a puppy here and a puppy there in her efforts to find, in her eyes, a safer place. The problem then arises of eclampsia.

The dimensions I have suggested will contain the bitch and the puppies, who cannot wander too far away from her, and out of the range of the heat lamp, and she does not have to worry about losing them in a large space. A contented bitch makes a good mum and this makes for a settled and healthy litter. The bitch should have a chance to get used to the whelping box before she is due to whelp.

THE ABSENCE OF PIG RAILS

You will notice from the drawing of the whelping box in this chapter that there are no pig rails. Pig rails are for pigs! They are not necessary, because the feeding of piglets is so different from that of puppies. A sow, as the female pig is known, weighs in at some 175lbs in weight. To feed her piglets she must get down and lie completely flat. The sow, from the day of her birth, spends her time on her feet, walking around and seeking food. This facility is not always made available to her, but this is her natural life style. To get her great weight into a lying flat position, she will drop onto her knees and then she simply flops down flat. One can imagine what happens to small piglets, who are able to run around at birth, should they be on the wrong side of mum when she drops. The pig rail delays her body making contact with the ground and, therefore, gives the youngsters more time to escape and get onto the right side of mum.

THE NUMBER OF TEATS

The sow's milk is not on tap all the time, but needs to be pumped out by her. So piglets get nothing at any other time and are never seen hanging on to mum, as puppies often do. This makes the number of teats that a sow has very important, for she can only rear the number of young that she has teats for. This is not the case with the bitch. Many owners and first-time breeders do worry that, because their bitch only appears to have eight, or even fewer, nipples, they will be in trouble should the bitch have, for example, ten puppies. This certainly is not the case. A bitch of any breed will have milk available all the time and it is a well-known fact that some puppies will be feeding whilst others are soundly sleeping. I have a bitch, whom I describe later in this chapter, who has had mastitis in two of her glands, which are now not functioning at all, yet with her remaining five she is doing very nicely, rearing a greater number of pups than she has nipples. All are always content.

HEAT AND DRAUGHTS

Your whelping box should be in a room free from draughts. More puppies die because of draughts than ever they do of cold. Do not have any other heating on in the room: your overhead heat lamp will be all that is necessary. I arrange my lamp to one side of my box, giving my bitch the choice of being able to lie where it is cooler, should she prefer. Some breeders prefer a heat pad, but I would rather have something I am more in control of, something that I can see immediately if it fails! Arrange the hanging lamp so as to make the bed temperature 70 degrees.

NEWSPAPERS

You will also need a large pile of newspapers. These are to place inside the box for the puppies to be born onto. Newspaper is warm and soaks up all the fluids which are lost during whelping. Use a good amount, several layers thick. Your bitch may make an effort to rip them up, while making her bed. Allow her to do so, it is part of her natural instincts.

As the bitch produces each puppy, there will be a massive loss of fluid. Simply mop this up by placing more newspaper and, sometimes, one can anticipate the next arrival and have the newspaper there first! Do not remove these papers; they can be safely left for several days. They provide a good source of warmth and, having been wet, they tend to dry slightly to the shape of the box and the bitch's body shape, making for safe havens for the tiny puppies, whose efforts to crawl will need something firm underneath on which to gain purchase. At, or before, but not later, than three days, when dew-claws have been removed, the bedding can be changed. I prefer vet-bed rather than old blankets. Vet-bed allows drainage and keeps puppies dry and, because it is of a stiff nature, it does not rumple up and allow puppies to wriggle underneath, thus running the risk of getting sat on by mum!

No bitch lies on her puppies deliberately, unless there is a problem, which I will go into further on. If puppies are found dead, and appear squashed, it is a greater possibility that they were already dead when they were sat upon.

KEEPING RECORDS

Another requirement is a pencil and paper and a watch or clock. It is important, and useful for future reference, that each puppy's time of birth be recorded, together with facts about sex and weight. If there is some way of identification, for example white toes, or a splash of white on the chest, then make a note of this so as to be able to identify each one on another day. The time of birth is important because, should the bitch go longer than two hours between puppies, then you need a vet, as it is likely she has one stuck. The weights are useful to know, as weighing could take place each day and any one which is slower to gain weight could have a deficiency, which your vet may be able to assist with.

TRANSPORT IF NECESSARY

Make sure, before whelping has begun, that the car has petrol and is furnished with clean vet-bed and that you know the emergency vet's number, in case you need to telephone him at night. Should there be a problem, it is better to take the bitch without the puppies she may have already given birth to. These can remain behind, they will be perfectly fine with the heat from the lamp until mum returns. A bitch's milk does not properly come down for twenty-four hours, and then some take a further twelve hours before it is in full flow, so pups left behind do not require any feeding of any sort – they will wait. Should any puppies be born, and then appear to be fading, it is not a good idea to start doing anything with them other than to make sure they are warm. With some puppies even a heat lamp does not appear to help. Any dead puppy should be referred to your vet – he will know whether to treat the bitch, or the remaining litter, or not. Very tiny puppies should not be bottle fed in a vain attempt to keep them alive. I am of the belief that, as I have offered every opportunity for the bitch to rear this litter, then those who cannot make it must have other problems. I do know of a breeder who bottle-fed a tiny one, but still the puppy never made a proper-sized dog and the people who bought the puppy were at the vet's all the time. This was a dog just not destined to survive.

USING A THERMOMETER

I have mentioned many things which you will need, and the reason for them, but what you will really be asking is how to know when whelping starts. This is where a thermometer plays its part. I do not have any sympathy with breeders who say: "I've been up all week with this bitch and she had the puppies when I fell asleep." My advice is, when your bitch has carried the pregnancy for eight weeks, start taking her temperature every night and every morning, by inserting the thermometer in her anus, and record it on your calendar, or somewhere easy to see. Her normal temperature will be 101.5 degrees to 102 degrees, higher than human beings. When the first stage of her labour begins, her temperature will drop. Each bitch, as I have said before, is different, and it may drop as low as 95 degrees.

The dropping of the temperature will take up to twelve hours, so if it is normal when taken at night, then you can go to bed and rest. If you find it has started to drop in the morning, then you have time to do all your other chores before you will be needed to sit with the brood bitch.

EARLY LABOUR

This will usually be marked by heavy panting, so heavy that one may suppose that she has just had a mile gallop. I do not get my bitches into the box at this stage, as it can be quite a lengthy procedure, and I get tired of sitting and waiting. I wait, usually doing some odd job, and I find that the bitch tends to follow me about, until I see her have a contraction. This may be seen as a holding of breath, while a ripple runs down her back. It is at this point I take her to where my whelping box is placed.

AVOIDING UTERINE INERTIA

Not all bitches follow this pattern. It may be that your bitch will not have a stage of panting but go from the fall in temperature right into labour, as we humans know it. There is, however, something which all should beware of and that is, if the bitch is not satisfied that there is anywhere suitable for her to give birth to her young, it is possible for her to hang on to them whilst she is undecided – and here we have uterine inertia. This is a condition where the cervix, having dilated to allow the passage of the puppies to the outside world, then goes into reverse and prevents the birth. Hence the need for checking and timing the arrival of each whelp. I know of two Gordons whose owners have just experienced this event: both were first-time breeders and, but for the intervention of myself, might well have lost their bitches. One had done all the correct procedures, prepared a room with whelping box and heat lamp, started to take the bitch's temperature, recorded it carefully and then, instead of taking the bitch to the whelping box, if needs be on a lead, they carried on doing their jobs and waiting. The bitch tried to make a bed between two armchairs. This was stopped by putting a piece of furniture in the place to prevent damage to the carpet. Eventually the bitch gave up and, when I enquired two days later how the puppies were, I was horrified to hear this story and find that the pups had not yet arrived. I advised immediate veterinary attention. The outcome was that a caesarian operation was performed: five pups had died, five were retrieved, but one of these only lasted twenty-four hours. What a waste of puppies!

The second case was of a bitch who was an adoring pet, and lived in the house with complete freedom of movement. She normally slept on her owner's bed but, when it came time to whelp, she was put outside into a stable, in January, and only had a bed of straw with an ordinary 60 watt bulb suspended overhead. The result here was the same. When left on her own she made so much noise that her owner went down the garden to the stable and opened the door to remonstrate with her. The bitch shot past her and, as it was dark and at night, dropped a pup on the garden path. By the time I arrived this bitch had been trying to produce her litter for some twenty-four hours and it was obvious that she was now in the stage of uterine inertia. Again there was a caesarian and again, half the litter had already died.

CORRECT WHELPING PROCEDURE
My advice is, when the temperature is right down, take your bitch to the whelping box she has been introduced to earlier. Place plenty of newspaper in it and stay with her, encouraging her to make her bed. Once she has had the first puppy she will not leave the box but, unless she has experienced this procedure before, she will look to you for support one way or another.

Once there is any discharge from her vagina, I make note of the time just in case the first one is a problem, but normally the first sight of fluid is very quickly followed by a puppy. On its arrival, in spite of the bitch's attention, I always ensure that the membrane, which all are born in, is clear of mouth and nostrils; after this I leave everything to my 'mum' to deal with. Should this be a maiden bitch, she may not, at first, chew away at the umbilical cord to separate it from the placenta or afterbirth. Should this happen, then I never touch it until the next whelp has arrived and then I cut it with a sterilised pair of scissors while she attempts to clean up the new arrival. She usually gets the message after the first two or three have been born. I cut the cord near to the placenta; the bitches often worry the breeder as they appear to be chewing the cord too near to puppy's tummy. Try not to interfere – puppies are tougher than you think.

DEALING WITH ECLAMPSIA
This condition is mostly hereditary and these bitches should never be bred from, to prevent any further cases. It is caused by the failure of the bitch to absorb and retain calcium. The result is that, when the bitch is feeding her puppies, she has no control over what they take, or what her body allows them to have, and they will take all the calcium she has. The effect on her is that she has little memory of what and where she is and will attack her puppies, often fatally, presuming them to be some kind of enemy.

It is often the case that this condition is not evident until the puppies are approaching three weeks of age, when the milk supply is at its greatest for quality and quantity. With each subsequent litter the onset is earlier and earlier. Many whelps die, sometimes whole litters, especially when breeders do not understand what it is or do not wish to consult their vet. The remedy is simple enough, but veterinary advice must be sought immediately. Injections of calcium at regular intervals and in advised doses will keep everything on an even keel, but attention to detail is a 'must'. Hopefully breeders will not allow their greed for finance to overcome the need to spay the bitch and place her in a pet home. Eclampsia can occur immediately after giving birth, but this is rare.

I have been quite horrified at breeders' explanations and actions taken when this has occurred in their kennel. One said that she heard the noise from the kennels and found the bitch attacking the whelps, some of which were already dead. She moved the bitch out and brought the puppies into the house. She told me that later that day she had heard the bitch crying for her puppies but she said: "I let her pay for the damage, I hope the huge supply of milk made her as uncomfortable as it could." What a way to reward an animal for its services to humans – a bitch with no recollection of her own actions and certainly no knowledge as to why it all took place and why the puppies were crying and bleeding!

Another breeder kept her bitch and puppies in her bedroom so as to prevent any further damage but, as soon as they were old enough to feed for themselves, she removed the mother and "flung her down the kennels. I never want to see her again." Neither of these took veterinary advice, and the latter sold on the remainder of this litter to buyers, with no instructions about not breeding from the females. This particular bitch had a mother who had displayed the same pattern of behaviour.

We have a lot to answer for, as breeders, for we are the caretakers of the breed, hoping to see it safely move into the hands of the next generation. Some will have a lot to redeem.

THE FIRST FEW DAYS

The first few days after the birth can be a tricky period, especially if the breeder is experiencing whelping their first litter and it is a first time for the bitch. I am a great believer in putting a lot of trust in my bitch and in her instincts. The process of giving birth is quite a traumatic experience for the whelps, who may take a great deal of time to make their debut into society. Nature, however, has already cushioned them to deal with this experience and they are far more hardy than we give them credit for. Yet even so, there are losses of young. Usually this happens within the first three days of life. There are, indeed, many reasons for the loss of young whelps, but breeders would be wrong to assume that every dead pup has been laid upon by its mother. It is my belief that bitches only ever lie on pups which are already dead. Unless I lose one through the pup's own inability to survive due to being very weak at birth or extremely light in weight, or for a reason I can see and understand, then, should I experience dying pups, I consult my vet at the very first loss. I have experienced what is commonly called 'fading puppy syndrome'. It cost me five whelps from a litter of eight – in fact I lost every bitch. Since that time I am more vigilant than ever during those early days. The symptoms of this fade are rapid dehydration, which then brings on hypothermia, after which death is very quick. In spite of efforts to revive pups, once they have lost body heat, it seems impossible. I now keep a special preparation in my drug cupboard in readiness for each litter, which at least stops the dehydration.

A contented bitch with her family, now a week old.

A sightless pup uses its nose to make its way to its mother. The puppies snuggle together for warmth and companionship.

Another cause can be damage from a very disturbed bitch who is either too hot or too cold, or maybe even feeling that the place she is made to whelp in is not secure. I have seen folk who have expected their bitch to whelp in the kitchen, which is no more than a public thoroughfare, everyone using this way to gain access to the house! A bitch that is too hot, due to incorrect height of the lamp, may well try to cover her young to protect them. She may also revert to this scrabbling if she feels that they are too cold or in a draught. So it is important to pay attention to these details before the whelping procedure begins. Remember, get a household thermometer and arrange the lamp so that the bed is 70 degrees F and no more! It is fairly important that the bitch gets well exercised after the birth. She may seem restless after two or three days have elapsed. If it is her first litter she may be reluctant to leave her new family, but it is important that she fulfils her bodily functions as soon as possible after whelping, the next day at the very latest. We must also remember that, if she were wild, she would need to hunt for food within a week, so make sure that her restlessness is not a desire for more rigorous exercise. Unlike humans, galloping will promote her milk supply, providing that she is correctly fed.

THE PROBLEMS OF A DOUBLE MATING

There is also the case of the bitch who has been mated twice, with a considerable time – a number of days – between the two alliances. This can happen when an owner, who also has a male, does not realise that his bitch is in season. When he does, he separates her from his own male, as he wishes to mate her using another dog who lives elsewhere.

Dogs and bitches who live together know each other very well and the bitch chooses her mate some six weeks before she actually looks as if she is in season. Therefore, it has been known that a bitch will allow a dog she knows well, or who is the chosen one, to mate her very early in her season, quite often while she is still showing colour. If, then, she is mated to another dog when her owner assumes it is the correct time, then there are going to be two separate conceptions and ultimately two separate litters.

The problem which arises is that the eldest crop of puppies will commence the procedure of birth when they are ready and cause the early arrival of the results of the second mating. The eldest and strongest will survive but the younger lot may find existing very difficult as, if they are premature, it is quite likely that there will be no instinct to suckle, this being one of the last instincts to be implanted into the unborn foetus. Unless the breeder is prepared to feed these unfortunates with a dropper, it is most likely that they will die. The whelps resulting from the early mating are possibly in small numbers – one, or perhaps two, pups – and the greatest number will come from the second mating, when all the eggs had descended into the womb. So this kind of carelessness, on the part of any breeder, is costly in time and effort, particularly for the bitch. It would be better had the whole event been aborted and a proper mating taken place the next time the bitch came into season.

DROPPER FEEDING

Feeding with a dropper is an exhausting business for the breeder and can only really be achieved by involving many other people, who can form a rota to ensure that a strict timetable of feeds is adhered to. Each puppy will require a meal every two hours, as will any orphan puppies, should anyone be unlucky enough to lose their bitch during whelping. It takes quite a few minutes to feed each puppy, so it is better if two people are rostered together. This makes for good company, especially throughout the night, and two pairs of hands can be better than one.

MATERNAL CARE

Everyone who has ever had a litter, or observed a bitch with her very young pups, will be very aware of how much attention she gives them, especially in those very early days. She seems to spend most of her time licking them. This licking is very important to their survival, for it is not until they are some two to three weeks of age that they are able to have any muscle use of their bladder and anus. It is these constant efforts by the bitch which cause them to defecate and urinate. Without her, this function could not take place. Anyone trying to rear an orphaned litter must use either a piece of towelling or a flannel, or some kind of rough material and constantly imitate the bitch's tongue, with similar movements of the flannel, otherwise the puppies will not empty themselves, which leads to blockages and infection, and their survival rate will be nil.

This constant licking, which the nursing bitch inflicts upon her young is, of course, very necessary at the moment of birth. If allowed, she will clear any membrane away from the pup's head and the strength of her tongue also improves circulation, encourages the heart to take up its function and generally raises the pup's temperature which, in turn, dries them thoroughly. Unless there is some trauma which causes us, as breeders, to take over even if only for a short time, we will never appreciate just how hard these nursing bitches work in their efforts to care for their young.

Such a situation arose with one of my bitches. As I only live in an ordinary house – although it sometimes resembles a large kennel in which I live with the dogs – and my two children have fled the nest, having nests of their own, I whelp my bitches in a spare bedroom. This means that the bitch has to negotiate a flight of stairs. My house is of split-level design, with the lounge upstairs. Therefore it is easy to assume that all my dogs, as they live indoors for most of the time, will be quite used to this activity.

The stairs are of the barn type, that is to say, they are open and the only hand rail is attached to the wall. Quite a daunting experience for a dog who has never been asked to get him or herself to another level. A three-year-old bitch, by the name of Britzka, was in whelp for the first time, and it was not until the time had arrived when it was necessary for me to get her into this bedroom to allow whelping to happen, that I realised that I had never seen her in the lounge. I climbed up about five stairs and called her – but no, she was not coming, although she seemed eager to be with me. I fetched a lead and, holding it quite close to her, attempted to get her to go alongside me. This, I am pleased to say, worked and, although very gingerly, she made it to the bedroom. I do have a wrought-iron ornate gate at the top of the stairs as there are always going to be times when I need to keep the Gordons out, especially if I have visitors who are not keen on dogs!

After Britzka had whelped, the older bitches were very interested in the muted sounds which their acute hearing could pick up. The gate had to remain shut, as, had the older girls managed to get upstairs, I knew they would be clever enough to open the door to see these new arrivals. This would have meant disaster, because I had gone against dog lore by mating a younger bitch and, therefore, she would be resented and, quite possibly, punished. So the gate was carefully closed after each visit to the new family and, of course, Britzka needed to negotiate the stairs on a daily basis and many times, at that, to fulfil her own daily ablutions. I was aware that, although she now made the trip unaided, she still was very wary of the whole idea.

When her whelps were about seven days old and she was now out at exercise with all of the other Gordons, we returned from our walk and, as usual, Britzka made her dash for the stairs. She raced to the top, only to find the gate was closed. Britzka, it seemed to me, did this stair dash in some vain effort to get it over quickly; so arriving at the top in top gear, as it were, completely threw her. Instead of stopping and waiting for me to open it, she turned in full flight to descend just as fast as she had gone up. Sadly she slipped as she turned and fell, her udder hitting every stair on the way down. Within twenty four hours she developed a temperature and I realised that she was heading for mastitis.

This all occurred on a Saturday morning. I rang my vet and, yes, there was someone on duty. Her temperature was 105 degrees, she was quite obviously very ill. Two of her glands were hot and swelling badly as I waited to see the vet. Antibiotics were prescribed and bathing of the affected glands was advised. It was also suggested that her milk supply may suffer and I should be prepared to supplement the feeding of the pups. I was able to obtain a supply of dried milk from my vet, and home I went.

By the time Sunday morning had arrived, the two affected glands were weeping and a porous condition was easily visible. I decided to place a dressing over them, which, of course, meant wrapping it right around the bitch's body. On Monday I arranged to see my own vet – the weekend had been attended by a locum. When he removed the dressing the two glands came away with the cotton wool leaving a large gaping hole. The vet took one look and said I would have to leave Britzka there, as he would need to close the hole with sutures. He assured me that I would be able to fetch her home later in the afternoon. Well, by this time the whelps were ten days old and looking well and I had not so far had to supplement the pups, but I knew that I was going to have to start then.

Feeding them was no problem at all. I had two bottles ready, so I could hold one in each hand, and two keeping warm in a jug full of hot water, so seeing to each puppy took less time. I felt very pleased with my idea until I arrived in the room clutching all this paraphernalia. I stared in horror. I had only been away less than two and a half hours but the state of the pups had to be seen to be believed! They were absolutely covered with faeces. That was not so bad; but, it wouldn't come off. It took masses of time spent on each one to get them clean and, of course, as soon as they were fed, they did it all over again! I certainly would not have liked to rear a litter of orphan puppies for the several weeks it needed until they were able to cope on their own. Although my bitch was so ill, I only had to supplement their food for a few days, as Britzka's milk returned and I was made redundant. Thank goodness for attentive bitches!

Britzka now has two milk glands that do not function any more, although one of the nipples was left intact, but she experienced no problems with her next litter.

THE FIRST FEW WEEKS

Having managed the mating and care of your bitch, you now have a new family to watch over and rear, hopefully to adulthood, or at least to stay in good health so that they may go to their new homes in tip-top condition.

For the first two and a half to three weeks the puppies will be content to lie snuggling next to mum, sleeping and sucking whenever they choose. Mum, however, must still receive your attention. Her newspaper must be changed for vet bed or a similar type of material.

Newspaper kept underneath it will allow the puppies' urine to drain away into it, but will need regular renewal. A thermometer on the wall will indicate the rise, or fall, of the room temperature. The heat lamp will need adjusting to maintain an even temperature which at floor level must not be allowed to rise higher than 70 degrees, otherwise the bitch will become uncomfortable and, in her efforts to look after her young, may try to cover them to keep the heat away. This can lead to injury, and even fatalities, as they become buried in the bedding.

Food for the nursing bitch should be increased as soon as her milk supply is readily available. I leave my bitches for two days before increasing their food intake, as they will have been fed quite normally up to this time and they will have been allowed to consume the placentas or afterbirth. As I wish to stick to nature's way, I try not to interfere with the bitch's wishes. At night, and throughout the hours of darkness, I leave the room unlit. The heat lamp will, of course, provide a dull red glow. I know that the bitch, in her natural habitat, would be living in darkness in a hole, either in the ground or in a dyke bank.

I increase the dam's meals slowly, taking a further two days to build up to a total of four daily. Breakfast consists of cereal and a little milk; meat, in my case, raw tripe – with added boneflour for lunch. She gets her normal ration at teatime, and supper depends entirely upon the number of puppies she is feeding. Should there be less than eight I would not consider supper as being necessary at all, although I would monitor her condition carefully, and feed as required.

DEW-CLAWS

Hopefully, dew-claws will have been removed. My Gordons all have their dew-claws removed at birth, if the bitch will allow me to handle them at that time, and certainly no later than at three days old. I use a pair of strong, slightly curved scissors for this and treat the remaining aperture with ground potassium permanganate.

I, personally, believe this is a must. Although the current laws in the UK do not allow puppies to be docked, they do not forbid the removal of dew-claws. We who breed must be aware that the majority of Gordon Setters raised are for sale to pet owners. While we hope they are going to good homes and, indeed, monitor the new owners where we can, we are very aware that the dogs will not get the meticulous attention that a show exhibit receives. This seeming lack of care is by no way intentional. Indeed, the show dog is only the recipient of this kind of treatment as it is so important to be seen in the show ring in tip-top condition. The important baths and coat trimmings mean the dog is handled more, and little things, such as claw-clipping, are done more often. The dew-claw, on an adult, eventually becomes hidden from view by the profusion of coat furnishing of the forelegs (Gordons never have hind dew-claws). In the pet home this claw may suffer neglect, on the basis that out-of-sight is out-of-mind!

Dogs in the wild, kennel dogs and those working on a daily basis over rugged crags and moorland will keep their claws well worn. The claws of a pet who lives indoors, possibly on plush floor coverings, will only wear in response to the surface on which the dog is exercised so the dew-claw will never come into contact with anything rough enough to wear it away. It will simply increase in length and often retain its sharp pointed end, which will inflict serious injury on anyone the dog may choose to jump up at; or it may continue to grow until it embeds itself in the animal's leg. On occasions, it may get caught up in furniture, or long grass and brambles, and get ripped out, causing a wound requiring, at the very least, attention each day or a visit to the vet.

SUPPLEMENTING MOTHER'S MILK

It is easy to know when the young need you to supplement their mother's milk, for you will become aware that they are a little noisy, not quite settled, perhaps even having a little moan, indicating they are not as comfortable as they have been. This is the time to offer food, usually at three weeks of age.

Some breeders start off by giving a thick milky substance, but I start with a small saucer full of minced raw bullock's tripe. A very flat plate would be as good. It needs something that they can crawl into and get covered in so as to encourage feeding. I keep the bitch away from them at this time, as she would quite happily steal their food. Since it takes the pups a long time to get the hang of eating, I tend to take the bitch out for a walk, to keep her occupied. I usually make the first offering an evening meal, then the puppies will sleep, as meat takes a long time to digest, and their dam will get a peaceful night's rest.

Unlike some domestic animals, a bitch's milk is there for the taking. A litter, consequently, is often seen with some suckling, and some sound asleep. As I have said, pigs, for example, lie down to feed their young and pump the milk through; they never feed whilst standing and only offer to feed for a certain number of times a day. That is why it is important that the number of young equals the number of teats, otherwise some will die, because they are not obtaining sufficient milk to sustain life. With the dog it is different, and this is why bottle feeding is so unnecessary, as all will get to feed at some time that day.

Later I introduce other feeds, making a daily total of four. I have even offered five meals daily to one particularly ravenous litter. I try to make two meals of cereal and two of meat. Although I may start with one feed being a milky one, I try to cut out milk as soon as possible. My reasoning for this is that milk they can get from their mother, so I do not need to supply it, and milk is something in which bacteria breed very easily, so I try to do without it as soon as possible. The range of complete dog foods offers a good variety of puppy food, but keep your eye on that protein level.

WORMING AND PROVIDING SPACE

At this stage of their development – three weeks – the pups will need their first dose of worming syrup, to be repeated every three weeks until they are six months of age. As they get older, the syrup can be changed for any of the other palatable wormers. These young pups will also need more space. The removable front to the whelping box can come out and a small puppy run added to this area. This will encourage them to come off their bedding to urinate and defaecate in the pen, so have it well covered with newspapers and change them many times a day. I always put the pups' food down in this area. I also make sure that there is an adequate supply of fresh water in a container that the pups will not knock over. Neither will it be so deep that they may drown in it!

At the age of five weeks the bitch's milk will have deteriorated, both in quality and

The nails of a three-week-old puppy are very sharp. They require regular trimming, otherwise the puppy will scratch the mother when it is feeding.

Gentle pressure on top of the pad will cause the claw to protrude, and this makes it easier to trim.

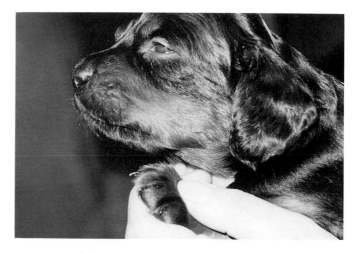

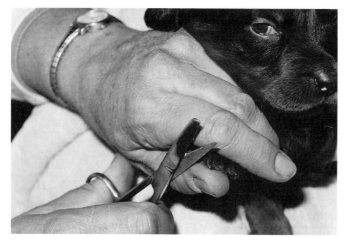

Round-ended surgical scissors should be used to trim the nails. Note that the left hand controls the puppy's head as well as the foot.

quantity, and she is liable to be most reluctant to feed the puppies, or even sleep with them. There should always have been a separate bed available for their mother, should she ever choose not to spend her time inside the box. I make sure that the sides of both the whelping box and the puppy run are constructed in such a way that these youngsters cannot escape, but I never deny the bitch her access, for I feel that this social contact is most important for the youngsters and the bitch. I allow this contact to continue until the pups go to their new home and, if I am keeping one, then access is never denied.

The puppies' claws will often get so sharp as to damage the bitch's udder considerably. The growth should be carefully monitored so that the bitch does not become unwilling to feed them. At any time after two weeks of age, these claws can be shortened very easily with a pair of scissors, but beware about cutting into the quick.

COMMON AILMENTS

Once the litter is born, it does not necessarily follow that all these new arrivals will sail through to adulthood without mishap or, indeed, will live to eight weeks of age. There are many pitfalls along the way. The ones I choose to mention are conditions which I have witnessed, although there are some that I have never had to nurse, but I am aware that they do exist within the breed.

There are many 'shunts' which can occur and one is hepatic shunt. The term 'shunt' simply means misplaced, or not where it should be. As to hepatic shunt, I had this condition occur in one whelp in a four-week-old litter. The symptoms were lethargy accompanied by extreme lack of colour in the mouth and gums, an anaemic condition by appearance. This pup was put to sleep, as there was nothing but pain and death ahead. It is not an hereditary condition but rather congenital. The other one, which also happened to me, was a bitch puppy who was lively, ate well, had a wonderful temperament, yet did not keep up the same pattern of growth as her litter mates. Eventually I gave her away at the age of sixteen weeks, to a very dear friend of mine, because she was the size of an eight week old. At twelve months my friend's vet took an interest, and realised that the great tube which carried the blood supply around the puppy whilst still in the womb, had not made its move to link up with the heart. Therefore, her heart was growing rapidly and almost filling the chest cavity. The vet was sure that an operation would put this condition right. My friend agreed, but the bitch, sadly, died on the operating table, because the tube simply disintegrated. Maybe things would have been different had the operation been done earlier: who knows?

Sometimes it is the case that the nursing bitch rejects one of her pups. People will say she pushed it away, but this is not really what happens. The bitch, sensing that there is a problem, does not wish to rear that puppy, and her reaction is to keep moving around her nest in the knowledge that the healthy ones will smell where she is and move after her. Young pups, treated in this manner, rarely last longer than three days. I leave mine until they are foundering, only removing them when the bitch is out of sight.

Other ailments that usually occur at five to six weeks of age are known as 'Puppy Head Gland Disease' and 'Juvenile Pyoderma'. These two are not the same illness, although they do get confused. Puppy Head Gland disease is exactly what it states. It only affects the very young: symptoms are swelling of the glands in the neck and head. This can be so gross as to cause the puppy to resemble something of a monster. Eating is difficult because of the swellings inside the mouth, but the pup, apart from being horrendous to look at, does not appear ill. The puppy will still greet you every morning with a wagging tail, although the head is so swollen that the eyes are no longer visible. This condition is caused by a staphylococcus, of which there are many types. A scraping is taken from one of the many suppurations and a culture grown. This, of course, takes some eight to ten days, which means the condition has time to get worse. Once the culture has established the identification of the staphylococci, then drugs can be administered that will have the desired effect. A broad-based antibiotic is used in the meantime.

Many veterinary papers have been written on this problem but, because it is not life-threatening, no real studies have been carried out. It is now assumed to be hereditary, taking the form of a lack of inborn immunity. Sometimes only one whelp is affected, with the others living quite happily alongside the problem. Certainly, those affected, although they do recover, should never be bred from.

Juvenile Pyoderma is an allergy and used to be referred to as puppy milk spots, as this is the form it takes, with small pustules appearing along the lower lip edge and around the jaw. I have heard vets mention that the pup is allergic to something carried on the mother's skin. However, they grow out of it, with little to show that they have ever had it, whereas the head gland disorder leaves severe scarring on the face and muzzle. It seems that, wherever the glands have erupted, the hair never grows back, as the follicles have been destroyed.

Immunity plays a most important part in the rearing of a puppy. The very young whelp should be protected by the mother's immunity which she passed on before birth, but if she has none, or very little, then anything she breeds will have problems. It is well known that each whelp is covered by the bitch's immunity until somewhere between eleven and twelve weeks of age, by which time it has disappeared. Therefore inoculations before this date are quite liable to render the pup with no protection at all, as the mother's immunity will have wiped the inoculation right out. So the time to get vaccinations done is all-important. Puppies' immunity levels can be also be lowered at other times, through teething and illness

If you keep your head, think carefully and are lucky, you may become a successful breeder, but it is unlikely that fate will always be on your side!

Chapter Eight

CARING FOR PUPPIES

Once food has been introduced, I never deny my bitch access to her pups, except when they are eating. I believe that this time, from five weeks onward, is the time of learning from mother. The bitch herself will probably appear to be unwilling to lie to feed her young, but she will nonetheless keep in constant contact with them. This is when she teaches them the difference between behaviour she will accept and behaviour she will not tolerate – and the consequences if they get it wrong. I make sure that she has access to them whenever she chooses. This is easily achieved by making an obstacle, which she can get over, but the pups cannot. Eventually they will disappear to their new homes and, provided they do not all go on the same day, the bitch seems to accept the loss without too much distress. Yet, before this age, I have known breeders who totally removed bitches from their young, causing great distress and, in one case, a bitch severely injured herself in her efforts to get back to her young. So do take care and think carefully about any actions you may decide upon. It is wonderful, when the bulk of the litter has gone, to sit and observe, without interference, the rapport between the bitch and her young. One can see the lessons being taught and the way in which the young are warned when they have gone too far, by the rough treatment from their mother.

PRESERVING THE PECKING ORDER
Here, in my domain, the only adult allowed to play with the puppy is their mum. I do not subject my other adults to the pranks of someone else's children. Why should they put up with this behaviour? This way, I never run the risk of getting my puppy bitten. I know that I have said elsewhere that the bitch will protect her young from the unwelcome advances of an older dog, but the case may be that I have broken dog lore by having bred from a younger bitch, whilst her elders and betters are still present. She may, therefore, get a browbeating from her mother, and whilst she would grovel and accept her punishment, someone else could be doing the same to her puppy. The rule is: "Never allow your puppy to get bitten." This is the responsibility of every breeder. I have heard the most terrible advice meted out to new owners by people who should know better but, obviously, have never taken the time to learn.

One breeder sold an eight-week-old puppy to a couple who already had a three-year-old male. The advice was to mix this puppy with the adult before the adult was four years old, as he may not accept the pup after this age. Well, the outcome of this was that the puppy endured several visits to the vet for stitches, skull damage and various other injuries. The new owners went on with this treatment of the pup until advised differently. I never allow any dog, except mum, to mix with my youngsters until they have become aware of the difference between their mum and other canines. Then they will have learned the art of what is seen as grovelling, but is actually submitting to the older dogs' authority, by lying down in front of them. This usually occurs at about seven to eight months.

NEWSPAPER TRAINING

Gordon Setter puppies grow very rapidly and, if they are to make healthy adults, then considerable care is necessary to ensure that all goes smoothly. As I have given them a small run whilst they were still with mother, they will have learned to use one, together with the newspaper in it on which to defaecate. This will become a useful tip when the young go on to their new homes, for a piece of newspaper can be used to control the area which it is desirable for the pup to use as a toilet.

FEEDING

Feeding is all-important, as it is just as damaging to overfeed as it is to underfeed. Overfeeding, with the odd exception, is difficult to do, but much damage can be done by the use of too much protein. There are some breeds that are not affected by this method of feeding, but there are many tragedies to be seen in Gordon Setters because of an owner thinking that they were doing the best for their puppy. As previously stated I never feed any higher than 27% protein and, for puppies, I believe that 25% is sufficient. I have experienced pups with osteoporosis. This is the name for a condition caused by feeding too much protein at the expense of other essential nutrients.

The symptoms are lameness, accompanied by pain, sometimes an unwillingness to stand up, and often large swellings around the joints. The condition is caused by an inability to absorb the protein in the diet and it has the same effect on the pup as rickets. I know of many Gordons who have suffered in this way, due entirely to the food intake.

My way of feeding is to offer four feeds a day at first, two of cereal and two of meat, and allowing the pups to eat as much as possible in fifteen minutes, after which time the bowl is removed. I have never experienced pups which were too fat, for as soon as they reach the age of eight to ten weeks, they become so active that they use the food in energy rather than store it as fat. Sooner or later one of these feeds will be rejected: sometimes it is the midday feed and sometimes it is the early afternoon one. Whichever it is, and it will be the pup's choice, I still give the other three meals on the same basis – that is, as much food as possible to eat in fifteen minutes. Of course, this will result in meals getting larger. A limit is put on, usually when the pup is about twelve to fourteen months of age, earlier in bitches, and this is when a total intake of two pounds of meat per day per pup has been reached. I do not like exceeding this figure. At about eighteen months for bitches, but much later in males, I start to cut down on the food, keeping an eye on their condition all the time. Males take a lot more food than bitches without getting too fat. As these young ones grow, the feeds per day become just two and I usually stick to this number, even for adults.

I know that there are many complete foods available, and once adulthood is reached, one of these may prove to be more convenient to use. I use these with my own dogs, but I do prefer some meat for my puppies and growing stock. If a complete food is used, there is no need to add any supplements, as the food will have been engineered to a dog's needs.

If you are not using a complete food, then additives will be needed and consultation with your vet will be of help, or use commonsense and purchase just one supplement. Do not try to feed more than one, as this will lead to too much being offered to the puppy and you will soon be back to a rickets situation, as this is what happens when you overdo the additives: it can keep the bone growth down, not encourage it.

SOCIALISING

Socialising is an important factor in the rearing of a Gordon pup. I will always take back any puppy I have bred, whatever the age, should the owners no longer want the dog. This is something that I instil into all new owners who buy their pups from me. I have noticed that those whose socialisation was left to pure chance are those whom society may label as having a bad temperament. I will not accept that there is any dog who is born bad: any deficiency is simply the result of being failed by humans.

It is important to socialise your Gordon puppy at a very early age, for it is imperative that a bond with the handler is formed as early as possible. The Guide Dogs for the Blind Society advocates sending their puppies to new homes at the tender age of six weeks and also insist that they are taken into the public eye from that time. It has long been thought that, at six weeks of age, there is less trauma involved than if the pup changes hands at an older age. I can personally support this observation. When I look back at pups that, for any reason, have been forced to meet society at an earlier age than eight weeks, for example for veterinary treatment, I realise that all of these are extrovert by nature, almost to the point of being hyperactive. They abound with energy, rushing to greet everyone who comes towards them, whether this be a dog, child, adult, horse or cow. They are actually in danger of being bitten, because they are so demonstrative. Yet others that I see sometimes not getting socialised until fifteen or sixteen weeks, are often too shy to deal with and seem to become more timid as efforts are made to introduce them to society.

To produce the desired temperament, everything must be taught. The best method is by ensuring that, whenever you are with the puppy, you give constant supervision and instruction, no matter what the age. As it is not wise to exercise the young ones with adult Gordons, then a simple obedience class is useful, both for the owner and for the pup, who can socialise as well as learn.

THE COLLAR AND LEAD

The very first lesson for the youngster is learning to accept a collar and lead. This is easily done by fastening a collar around the puppy's neck for a day or two. Make sure that the collar is neither too loose nor too tight. The puppy will scratch at this intrusive thing at first, but eventually will accept it without a problem. The next move is to clip a lead on to the collar. This will need a lot of tact and diplomacy by the owner. Several different reactions may occur. The puppy may struggle, or pull away or try to flee. Whatever the reaction, the

leaving the puppy behind while she walked the older dog. Although I pointed out that the mess only happened at night, I could not change her mind. Her comment was: "He knows that he has done wrong, because he hides as soon as I open the door!"

I discovered that there had been a change in the diet of this youngster. My friend had been feeding the puppy tripe for two meals a day and cereal for the remaining one, but had changed to giving the puppy a complete food. Because she had noticed a weight loss in the pup, she had increased his food and he apparently had his last feed at ten o'clock and then was put into the kitchen to bed. Well, the bulk of this last feed was just too much for him to contain until morning and he was hiding every time the door opened because he expected to be beaten. I suggested that he had a meal of pure meat as his last feed: this takes longer for the body to deal with and should see him clean throughout the night. My friend was sceptical, but I asked that she follow my advice for just one week and then report back with the results. She telephoned after three days. Her words were: "You were exactly right." So here was another example of not quite understanding canine behaviour.

Another case of misunderstanding was when I rehoused a Gordon that had come into the 'Rescue' scheme. This little working bitch was just four years of age. My neighbour, with whom she was placed, was not truly a doggy person. By that I do not mean that she did not love dogs but rather that she expected them to behave, and to learn like children do, which is not what one should expect. Sometimes she would accompany me on the walks that I did. These consisted of some two to three miles, the dogs being off the lead for most of the time. We met outside my back garden gate and of course, Lottie, as this little bitch was named, promptly threw herself onto her back and grovelled to mine. I had seven Gordons of all ages with me and some exceeded Lottie in years. Therefore her instinct, in order not to be bitten or harassed by this mass, was to submit, so that there was no threat of harassment. My neighbour, however, was horrified: she poked the bitch with her foot, demanding that she stop being silly and get up. I do wonder how many dogs are treated in this way, or even more harshly, for what their owners consider an inconvenience. It does of course make their coats dirty, depending on the ground conditions at the time. However, this bitch was never going to find herself in trouble with other dogs!

Chapter Nine

TRAINING AND EXERCISE

Whatever the reason people have for purchasing a Gordon Setter, whether the dog is simply to be a companion, or be shown, or shot over, or entered in Field Trials, some form of training is required from the day the pup arrives in the new home.

The youngster has been removed from the mother and therefore has lost that vital mentor, companion and tutor. The pup will feel very lost and will be looking for someone to become attached to for safety and, hopefully, to learn from. Whatever the reason for buying the puppy, this person will be the one who tends to the puppy's needs, and provides the food. Remember, the new owner has the advantage, because the owner makes the arrangements about collecting the pup and therefore can be prepared; but the pup has no prior knowledge of this major disruption that is about to take place.

THE FIRST STEPS
My advice to those buyers who require a Gordon as a pet, is to find their local Canine Society, which will know where there are classes for purely Obedience or show ring training. Either of these will suit the new owner, as both will allow the puppy to socialise with other dogs who are under control. It will allow the new owner to witness the youngster's behaviour in the presence of others, and there will be someone to give advice should events take a turn for the worse.

EARLY SOCIALISING
Young Gordons do not need to be exercised at all until some muscle has been put up, and this is not liable to be before nine months of age. It is however, important to socialise. Attending dog classes is one way, but these meetings may only take place once a week, so more may be required. You can always take your puppy in the car to different places and ask all your friends, when you visit, if you can take the pup into the house to meet everyone. Take care if there is a resident dog, who may resent the youngster's intrusion, otherwise the pup could be bitten. There are two important rules which must be remembered at all times and they are: 'Never hit a Gordon' and 'Never let your Gordon pup get bitten'. These two rules are the most important lessons that owners will ever learn. It is essential to remember them well. As soon as the youngster is of an age to be lead-walked, it is important that the puppy sees heavy traffic, pedestrians, and whatever the road or path is carrying. The pup may react

Sh. Ch. Liric High Society: Winner of eight CCs and five Reserve CCs.
All Gordon Setters require a certain degree of training, whether you want a show dog, a working dog, or a companion.

T. Morgan.

in two ways, either by jumping up to greet everyone, or by retreating and trying to hide. Until this situation has been experienced, one is not to know which the reaction might be, so start by getting the pup to sit, while the people and their dogs go by. A gentle but restraining hand on the collar, coupled with a firm instruction to 'Sit', will prevent any unwanted reaction. When the path is clear, much social praise is all that is required. Never use tidbits at this stage; the pup will know when you are pleased.

This learned 'sitting' will be useful in later life, when the puppy has become a young adult. By automatically sitting when approached by other dogs, who may be loose or on a lead, your dog is less liable to receive a bad reaction from them. In this position no threat is being presented to their wellbeing and so there is less likelihood of any aggression.

I do keep stressing the importance of never letting your puppy get bitten. Your puppy's mother would never allow it to happen: she would be able to read all the signs, mostly body language which we humans would miss, and would thereby know when danger was lurking not too far away. She would remove her puppy from the scene, either by using her own body as a shield, or by making definite signals to the other dog to keep away. Not many males will take on a nursing bitch. Having taken this puppy from the nest at a very vulnerable age, we must be protective and be very alert on the puppy's behalf. Any puppy who comes off worst from meetings with other dogs before being taught to submit to them will, without question, start to growl at the sight of approaching dogs. The puppy is afraid and hopes that all the noise will ward off the other party. This is again where 'bad temperament' will start being mentioned, whereas it is the owner who should be protecting the puppy.

EXERCISE

The whole plan of exercise must be properly understood and here, as with any other part of the pup's day, routine is essential. Whilst it is important for the youngster to witness traffic and pedestrians, this must not lead to long walks. The puppy can travel by car and then get out to encounter the programme for that day – but no long walks until at least nine months of age. Young setters are full of energy and appear to be tireless yet, when observed closely, activity only comes in very short sharp bursts. Therefore I always advocate no lead-walking, except at training classes, until the puppy is at least nine months of age. This is to allow time for the skeleton to grow without injury. It is a well-known fact that more damage is done to hip joints between the ages of five and seven months than at any other time in a dog's life. Playing in the garden is enough. This does not prevent owners taking the youngster with them in the car to a friend's house to play and, in the case of those whose gardens are rather small, going in the car to a quiet park and sitting around while the puppy plays.

An adult will need to be off a lead, and free to gallop in a fenced area, at least once a day. Mine go twice, once early in the morning, and for a second, but shorter session, in the afternoon. This is because my garden is very small and does not afford much room for exercise, and because no dog likes to soil its own patch, so it is done away from home A walk of two miles is usually enough for any setter.

Do not allow the puppy to accompany older adults when first allowed to run loose, unless it is the puppy's mother, or an adult who is beyond the fast-galloping stage by virtue of age. Sometimes an older, but placid, dog can act as an anchor or homing-point for a young pup.

LEARNING TO COME WHEN CALLED

One word of warning: I hear many times from the owners of young setters that their dogs will not come back. They tell me that, whenever they call the dog's name, it is interpreted as a signal to turn and flee in the opposite direction. The owners seem to be of the opinion that the dog is deliberately trying to be difficult. There are two real reasons for this pattern of behaviour. The first is that the dog is short on exercise, in other words is not getting enough work and is reluctant to return, as this will be followed by the lead being replaced and the end of playtime. The other is a problem of youth. Until Gordons are about fourteen months of age, in some cases much older, they suffer from an inability to locate the direction of sound. So be warned, your dog may not know where the noise is coming from and will need to have visual contact to realise your whereabouts. And remember, your dog certainly will not return if you are then going to hand out chastisements or beatings, for being late!

I had an experience with one of mine, who was out for about the sixth time, on a very short loose walk, with some of my oldies. I am lucky in that I have a disused sand quarry, which is overgrown with bracken, heather and large broom bushes, only five hundred yards from my home. It is safe, away from roads, with tracks to follow, and wild rabbits, foxes and the odd covey of partridge, which make for good and interesting smells to any gundog. This young bitch was missing from sight as I neared the end of the exercise. I whistled her and, taking advantage of a high piece of ground, I scanned the view, awaiting her response. She came into view from behind a large broom bush, but appeared not to be looking in my direction, gazing instead away to the right of me. I blew my whistle again and she turned back and disappeared! I repeated the whole sequence and she did exactly the same thing each time – turned and ran away. She was, by this time, almost half a mile away and I began to worry. The next time she appeared I removed my scarf and waved it about and also jumped up and down. It worked, the movement had attracted her attention and, to my relief, she came at full gallop, as pleased to see me as I was to see her!

Many folk say that their dog won't come back. I wonder how many simply cannot, rather than won't!

GETTING USED TO OTHER DOGS

Should you have been careless enough to have allowed your youngster to get bitten, you may not actually see any resulting problems until the puppy is about twelve months old. Then the behaviour changes and your puppy will, on sight of another dog, start to grumble. This grumbling may not be loud enough to hear, but it can be felt, if a hand is laid on the dog. It will escalate, if allowed, because your dog is frightened and is attempting to ward off any approaching dog. The way to prevent this from occurring and to correct any signs of grumbling, is to be aware, when out with your Gordon, of what may take place next. Of course, if you are out with a puppy, you will be using the lead anyway, but the procedure is the same. Ask the dog to sit at your side. Show your support by placing a hand on the dog's head or gently take hold of the collar.

If you are quiet and instruct your dog to stay, remain in this position until the approaching dog has passed by, then praise your dog before giving the instruction to continue with the walk. The reasoning behind these instructions is that when two dogs meet, whether it is a dog and a bitch, two dogs or two bitches, vibes pass between the two animals which we humans have no way of detecting. If the dog sits, this is not a threatening stance when sighted by an approaching dog and therefore does not promote any interest. Do not try to move the other dog away. If your dog is unleashed, then there will be no problem. If you have suddenly put the lead on, then the reaction would be for your dog to jump up and down, making horrendous threatening noises, which may aggravate the other animal into attack.

I take out all of my Gordons, with the exception of young pups, all together. I would rather do this than go out many times in one day. Mine have two lengthy walks each day. I take off the leads once we are on the canal towpath, as it is bordered by fenced fields holding cattle,and the Gordons are all free to race off and gallop together. The towpath is only some ten feet wide in parts and is a popular place for many local inhabitants walking their dogs. One can imagine that other people, quite often with smaller dogs than Gordons, worry when they see seven galloping Gordons racing towards them, flews flying and teeth resembling a grinning ghoul – not a pretty sight. These folk invariably make the mistake of fastening their leashes back on to their dog, whose immediate response is to pull, making a throttling sound, or bark and scream, which could excite mine into some reaction. However, my Gordons have all been taught to sit and allow others to pass without incident. I train each youngster to adopt this behaviour when the time comes for joining the adults for walks.

AN EXAMPLE OF GOOD TRAINING
One day, the wind was blowing and it unexpectedly started to rain. I was wearing a parka-type coat, and I pulled up the hood which was fastened to the back of my coat, and tugged it well forward so that it could not be removed by the wind. With my head bent against the gale, I really only had a view of my feet and about three feet to the front of me. Suddenly I almost fell over one of my Gordons. I stopped and looked up, to find all were sitting down in a long line, close to the water's edge, for approaching was a man, accompanied by two Basset Hounds, who had already reached the first of my Gordons. The Bassetts sniffed and continued on their way, for their owner had not seen me either. Once past each other, all continued to enjoy their walk. Gordons are quick to learn and, once taught, do not need too many reminders.

TRAINING CLASSES
All Gordons, whether they are going to a pet home, or to be worked and shot over, or are destined for the show ring, must always have some time devoted to being in the company of others, especially their peers. There are three types of training available to ordinary folk. One of these is show handling classes, usually organised by the local dog club, to prepare a puppy in readiness for a show career. Here the youngster is handled by many people, gets lead practice and is given the opportunity to meet other dogs of all shapes and sizes. The puppy learns, while very young, that all this is acceptable and, as it is done in your company, you will take care to see that other dogs are not allowed to rough-house the puppy in any way.

There is also an Obedience class, again usually run by the local dog club. These are brilliant for folk who maybe have never had to be totally responsible for a dog of their own, although it is likely that they grew up with dogs. Obedience classes bring about a rapport with the dog and, whether they want to go on to serious Obedience, or simply want to be able to control their dog, these classes are invaluable. I advise all new owners, who have not had a Gordon before, to attend one class or the other.

The third class that would be available is for those who wish to use their dog to shoot over. There is a variety of Gundog Clubs. These run shows and also provide gundog training for many breeds. It is very easy to find regular classes for spaniels, and those breeds belonging to the Hunting, Pointing and Retrieving group. Setters, however, present a problem if you are really keen on actually competing in Field Trials. This problem is not always the lack of trainers but more a lack of ground over which to run. Whereas the other breeds can substitute dummies and, indeed start work with dummies until a good level of obedience is achieved, setters and pointers need a large expanse of land on which to train. They must quarter properly. Indeed great importance is attached to good quartering and there are prizes to be won for simply being good at it. One can imagine that, as each new dog goes out to learn quartering, a large piece of ground is needed and there are not too many farmers who can offer this facility. No Setter or Pointer will learn to work properly on ground that has no scent whatsoever. So the moors are the answer, you think! Sadly, in the UK, these are owned by great estates which rely on letting out shooting rights for large sums of money, and who would be unwilling to have their precious game disturbed or their sheep which graze the moor savaged by an out-of-control dog! However, all is not lost. There are now some societies in the UK that offer this kind of training outside the shooting season, by way of weekends on large estates. These can be useful and certainly they will indicate whether the dog has got what it takes to become a field trialler.

FIELD TRIALS
Although I have trained one of my Gordons for field trialling and ran her many times, I did not ever win an award, although I learned a lot about it, and I would never presume to have sufficient knowledge to give instructions here on how to train. There are other experts who have written books on this subject. Yet there is one piece of advice that I can give, which is that it is useless to send your dog away to be trained, for it is you who need to know how to do it. As with many things in life, each dog is only as good as the handler. Training a dog, for any purpose, builds up a rapport between handler and dog and this rapport is vitally important whether in competition or out shooting. This holds true for Obedience training as well. If you have handed over training to another person, and not attended the sessions yourself, then your dog will never work so well for you.

Chapter Ten

GENERAL HEALTH CARE

Gordon Setters need the same amount of care as any ordinary dog but with some special attention to detail in the areas associated with setter breeds in general.

EARS

Their ears are referred to as 'blanket' ears. This is because they hang down in such a way that they blank out, almost to exclusion, any air from the ear itself. Obviously, when out at exercise, the ears will move and allow some air inside, but generally the inside of the ear provides the humid conditions which tiny ear-mites just adore, because they thrive so well in it. Should you have a swimming Gordon, then water getting into the ear will exacerbate the problem.

The remedy for this condition is to wipe the ear out on a regular basis, even once a week will be enough, with either an appropriate ear wash, obtainable from your vet, or, if there is already a problem, with ear drops, again obtainable from the vet. Wax in the ear, once mites have become established, is seen as a very dark and odorous discharge. Should it be allowed to continue unchecked then, in very severe cases, it may be necessary to operate and fit a drain.

FEET

Feet are next on the list of priorities. The young pup and, indeed, some of the less well coated Gordons, will not need too much attention or time on the hair that grows between the dog's toes. The more profusely coated Gordon, however, will most certainly have feet which resemble floor mops, unless they are trimmed on a regular basis. Trim these by simply cutting the hair around the edge of each toe with a very good pair of scissors, preferably of the hairdressing type.

Having completed this task, place a finger between each toe and the next, dragging the hair outwards and upwards, and simply cut it level with the top of the foot. This will not only neaten the appearance of the foot but prevent the dog's feet from bringing mud and leaves into the house, carried by those great hairy feet!

In between the toes must be examined regularly to prevent the formation of matted hair, which can accumulate and perhaps pick up a thorn, or a piece of grit, which may become firmly lodged in the matted ball and cause extreme pain and soreness.

THE COAT

The coat, in general, needs brushing to stimulate the skin and promote further healthy growth. Care should be taken about washing or bathing the dog, because you must understand about the texture and the value of the coat to the dog. It is made up of hair which carries a certain amount of grease and oil. This oil is like a macintosh and prevents the skin from becoming completely soaked. Frequent bathing will interfere with the normal function of the coat's oils.

However, the family pet will need bathing occasionally, as will the show dog. The family pet, unless bathed regularly, will leave greasy marks when brushing against furniture, doorways, paintwork and, of course, sitting on chairs. Many Gordon lovers allow their dogs to sleep on their beds and so these animals will need more care than the outdoor dog. If it is necessary to bath your dog, you can obtain many animal shampoos from most pet shops but, always remember, you can improvise by using a very mild human shampoo, even those preparations that are intended for babies. Should you be one of those who does bath your Gordon regularly, please remember that, should your dog have been out in the rain, you must give a towelling rub-down to dry your pet off quickly and to create warmth, as the water may well have penetrated through to the skin. The show dog is always bathed on a regular basis immediately prior to each show, and will also receive many treatments to add lustre and life to enhance what is called show presence. But show exhibitors will be well acquainted with their dogs' needs.

NAILS

A dog whose main purpose in life is that of being a companion or pet will undoubtedly live in the house. In many parts of the world and, especially, in the UK, most homes have fitted carpets. This means that most of the dog's life, if calculated in days and hours, is spent walking or standing on soft floor-covering, affording no wear to the dog's nails at all. These will continue to grow, unless they are worn down, or because the dog is religiously receiving attention from a very caring owner.

I have many owners and friends who are afraid to trim their dog's nails for fear of cutting them back too far, thereby causing them to bleed and putting the dog in considerable pain. There are also many vets who are wary of dealing with Gordons' nails because they are black, and the quick is not as easy to see as it is in the white nail, which sometimes is almost opaque. However, this is no excuse for not attending to this very important part of your loyal member of the family.

I prefer to use the guillotine type of nail clipper, as this uses a paring motion and the weight-bearing surface of the nail can be gently shaved, sliver by sliver, until the centre appears to be becoming softer and starts to depress under the strength of the clippers. This is the time to stop. Never try to remove a large chunk of nail but, rather, shave it off. A large coarse rasp, very like the type used by a blacksmith on horses' hooves, is an ideal tool for those who are totally afraid to even try to use the guillotine. I must say that, once a dog has suffered a foot injury, for whatever reason, it will be difficult to handle them ever again, so maybe the rasp is better for the timid. When using one, employ a pushing motion, moving from the back of the claw towards the tip. Also, remember that, once the claw is the desired length, it can easily be maintained by just removing the smallest sliver once a week. Road walking is ideal for keeping a dog's feet and nails in good order but, quite often, there is insufficient time spent on this, particularly in the bad weather.

DEW-CLAWS

If your Gordon has dew-claws, these will need attention on a regular basis, for unless the dog is employed on search and rescue operations, working on craggy hills and moors, there will be no opportunity to do anything about the wear and tear of these peculiar nails. They can grow into the dog's leg if neglected and, should they grow too long, may get ripped out if they become caught in bramble, or thick undergrowth, while the dog is out at exercise. When I had horses, I acquired a Greyhound, purely to keep one of my youngsters company when out road-working – even horses need road work. This particular male was in preparation for Point to Pointing and he was so fit that he was nearly bursting out of his skin. The Greyhound accompanied him at exercise and the horse, instead of leaping on the passing traffic for fun, watched the Greyhound, who trotted quite quietly beside him until we were on open land where the dog often went completely mad for about five minutes, much to my horse's delight, as he was only looking for an excuse to have a lark. This Greyhound bitch was white, a retired racing dog complete with dew-claws. She often managed to rip them right out when having one of her mad flings and, of course, trotted home beside me with her ribs covered in blood. I lived in a village at this time and my neighbours were all country folk, mostly involved with farming and animal husbandry, so the sight of blood did not turn any heads, but I did get some odd looks in the early days until there had been time to answer questions as to why there was all this blood. This was all a few years ago, before video cameras, but we did have a cine camera which we used with the horses. One day I used it on the Greyhound and took some slow motion footage. I was amazed, when viewing later, to see just how the foreleg operated at a gallop: the whole of the back of the pastern descended flat onto the ground. No wonder she ripped her dew-claws out so often!

TRIMMING AND TIDYING FOR THE SHOW RING

As stated previously, the working outdoor dog will not need to be trimmed, although feet and ears and coat must be checked carefully. Most Gordons grow a very profuse ruff of hair around their necks. This can become untidy, particularly if the dog wears a collar continuously, which may cause hair to matt. A working dog must never have this ruff removed, as it affords protection against the brush and other foliage when the dog is running either in a Field Trial or through dense cover during hunting sessions. This sharp natural environment would simply rip the dog's neck to pieces after just one day's work. But, for the show specimen, or a dog whose owner prefers the elegant, clean look in the neck area, this ruff may quite reasonably be removed. It is usually done with thinning scissors or dog clippers, always working with the way that the hair grows. If this is carefully done, there is no need to expose any bare skin, and it gives the impression that this is a natural way to grow. Simply clear away the clump of hair that grows profusely at the base of the ear, then deal with the sides of the neck below the base of the ear and the front of the throat.

The part of the hind leg that is from the hock joint down to the back of the dog's heel

Sh. Ch. Lourdace Buccaneer of Benbreac (Northinch Briar of Keepersgate – Sh. Ch. Lourdace Grimalkin at Glenclova)

Peter Howard.

This Gordon Setter is typical of how the breed is shown in the UK with regard to shape and outline. Although this dog has his title, he was only lightly shown due to a back injury which recurred from time to time. However, he is trimmed in an ideal fashion. His body from the top of his back down to the commence of the belly feathering has been removed by hand, as have his flanks and slope of the shoulder blades. Clippers have been used to clear out his throat and the underside and underneath of his ears. Excess growth from the hock joint down to his feet has also been removed by hand. Removing by hand involves the finger and thumb plucking method.

This nine-month-old puppy shows the beginnings of a topknot.

An untrimmed top of the head, with the topknot growing profusely.

The topknot is removed by plucking out the hair with the finger and thumb.

The topknot has now been removed, leaving a smooth outline.

cushion, can have the sides, but only the sides, treated in the same manner as the neck. Using either thinning scissors, or clippers, and working in a downward action, gently remove the hair from the outside edge and the inside but not the back. If, having got this far, it can be seen that the hair down the back is still too long and thick, then this should be removed by the 'finger and thumb' method. All hair on animals grows for a purpose and, as with the horse, this hind leg hair acts as a drain for water, preventing it from soaking into the leg.

'Finger and thumb' is really a plucking action which, carried out correctly, simply takes away unwanted wool and gently thins and shortens without breaking. I use this method to remove hair from in between the toes. If it is done from puppyhood, or when it first becomes necessary, the dog quickly adjusts to the operation and it lasts for almost three months without too much attention, unlike scissoring, which, for the show ring, needs repeating each week. The same action should be taken to remove unwanted body coat. Too much clippering on the body would simply ruin the coat.

The Gordon Setter, unlike some other gundog breeds, does not have a moult as such. By this I mean that there is not a period where massive amounts of coat are shed in a very short

An untrimmed ear. Note the mass of hair at the base and underside of the ear, and the untidy throat.

The underside of the ear after unwanted hair has been removed, using thinning scissors or clippers. The throat has also been tidied up.

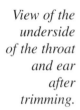

View of the underside of the throat and ear after trimming.

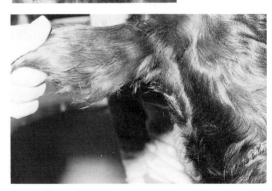

Cleaned out throat, viewed from the front.

Clippers are used to clear unnecessary hair from the back of the ear base.

View from behind the ear after trimming hair into the shape of the neck.

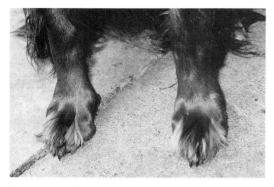

Untrimmed feet.

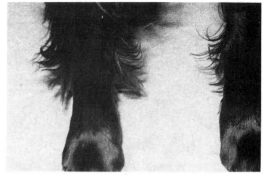

Trimmed feet. Note the correct oval shape.

Untrimmed fore-feet, viewed from the side. The untrimmed heel makes the foot appear flat.

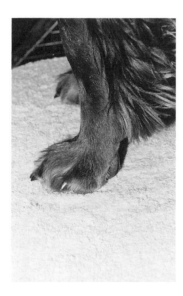

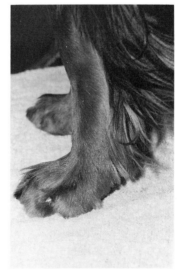

Trimmed fore-feet, viewed from the side. Note the hair from the heel has been removed.

time. Gordons' coats do shed, and are replaced, but not in the same fashion as the Golden Retriever or German Shepherd Dog. The Gordons appear to turn brown at the ends of the hair, which is very easy to remove; but the Gordon simply takes time and leaves bit of coat on bushes or heather, taking a long period to change it all, therefore not causing quite the same problems as other breeds. For showing purposes this coat would have to be removed some considerable time before it changed to a brown shade.

When a Gordon Setter is in the process of changing coat, it appears to lack sheen and lustre, and is referred to as being 'blown'. The changes take place in several stages; it starts with the head and neck, followed by the ribs and body, the croup and tail root being the very last place to become easy to remove. Sometimes it happens that the coat is all changed except the rear end and, indeed, this may take some removing as it is tough hair, but the dog will not look good until it has gone.

The places where the coat needs attention to enhance the dog's appearance, are entirely a

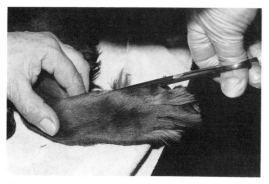

Trimming the side edge of the heel cushion.

Unwanted hair being removed from between the toes by plucking with finger and thumb. The rubber gloves afford a better grip on the hair.

matter for the owner. Personally, I remove clods from under the ears and from the front of the throat; fingerstrip the body and flanks and inside and out of the hocks and use scissors around the feet. This creates a stylish appearance, always showing in good coat. The top of the skull often grows with a tuft protruding from the centre; this is removed by finger and thumb and never, never cut.

BATHING

When bathing the dog, extreme care must be taken to remove all soap and any conditioner, if used. As most Gordons these days live in houses, bathing can become an unwanted chore for the owner, who may find it difficult to persuade the dog to get into the bath and then to stay there. Often owners are on their own, without any help at bath time, so it is easy to get into a mess: water everywhere and an uncooperative dog. There are dog baths on the market, which do not involve the heavy lifting of a Gordon, but these are for use outdoors and, while the sun shines and the weather is warm, they are wonderful; but in the rain, and with the wire carrying electricity, there could be problems. I bath mine out of doors just underneath my kitchen window. I have bought a fitting which attaches to my mixer tap in the kitchen and I use my garden hose through the window so I can control the temperature and really go to town with the amount of water. I do, of course, tie the dog to a ring that I have had fitted to the wall, to make the point that there is no escape. Dogs who didn't like the bath inside the house, probably through fear of slipping, simply stand outside with no qualms and no struggling, leaving both my hands free to get on with the washing process. I honestly believe that some dogs even like this method. The hosepipe certainly supplies the water quite fast, and has an almost massaging effect on the skin.

DRYING

To dry a dog, should you not have one of the expensive dryers seen at the many dog parlours, it is just as easy to use an ordinary hair dryer, one that has had a defuser fitted. Although this may take a little longer, yet it is a good method. I use this way of drying but I do have a grooming table, which allows me to work with the dog at a convenient height. When the dog is virtually dry, I use a huge bath sheet which I pin around the dog, using baby safety-pins. I pin the towel under the dog's chin and under the tail, after that I place an ordinary dog coat on top to hold the whole thing on. The dog wears this for about an hour.

I prefer to bath my dogs two days before the show, thereby giving the coat time to replace some of the natural oils the shampoo may have removed. A good brushing with a real hair brush (that is, one in which the bristles are actual hair) revitalises and cleans the coat; and the towel, replaced in the same manner as after bathing, works wonders when ready to show.

WORMING

Every dog, with whatever role in life and whatever living conditions, should be wormed on a regular basis. Puppies should be wormed regularly from birth until they are six months of age. This is important to rid them of roundworms, which can affect children unless proper hygiene is maintained. Worms mainly fall into two other categories – roundworms and tape worm. After six months of age I worm mine against roundworms every three months, all their lives, but I only worm against tape worms on veterinary advice. In Australia they need to worm daily, simply because a worm infestation had gone unchecked, in imported stock (not dogs), and they now have to take action against heart worms, whose larvae are carried by insects.

MEDICATION TO KEEP TO HAND

Every medicine cabinet for dogs should contain a thermometer. Using this to verify a rise in temperature often decides whether a visit to the vet is necessary or not. Dogs' temperatures vary slightly from dog to dog, from 101.5 degrees to 102 degrees, considerably higher than our own, so it is necessary to buy a thermometer with degrees numbered, rather than just the figure that we humans should register, as many of the modern ones show.

Whilst it is not in our interest to keep some medicines in stock, because they will lose their validity when they are out of date, some even becoming harmful, there is no reason why our medicine chest should not have some good standbys ready, should we need treatment and the vet isn't available or the time is not convenient. Mine contains some of the following: a mixture prepared by my vet to control diarrhoea, especially in very young pups. Given at the rate of fifteen-mil doses four times a day, the animal being starved at the same time, it can work wonders. I always keep a variety of ear drops in stock. I never manage to keep these long enough for them to become outdated. All these are aside from the normal wound powders, wound dressings, iodine, and elastic strapping; a variety of treatments for the removal of lice, fleas and ticks; antiseptic powders and sprays; and a very useful preparation for cut pads. Many do not realise that a cut pad will not knit its surface back together in the same way as skin involved in a wound grows back together. The hard surface of the dog's pad, although very different in appearance to the finger nail, responds in the same way. A damaged nail has to grow out, and a damaged pad surface has to grow from underneath to the surface. This is why a cut pad is seldom stitched up. The only time there may be cause for stitching is if the wound is so deep that the under-flesh requires some support to heal correctly. There are preparations which will help to fill a hole in a pad, preventing grit from entering.

Another must for the stock is a container of common washing crystals. These are to encourage a dog to vomit. We all grew up with the assumption that salt was the remedy for ridding the stomach of a foreign body. Salt is the most dangerous element one can use to encourage vomiting: it is an abrasive and, while it may succeed in obtaining the desired result, there may be devastating after-effects. As an abrasive, it does not return with the stomach content, but remains behind, and damages the stomach lining and the intestine. Should you become aware that your dog has just swallowed a foreign body, or you may be of the opinion that something has just been stolen which the dog thinks is food but which may be harmful, then a handful of washing crystals thrown down the back of the throat is a very fast remedy. My advice is to place the newspaper on the floor first because the response is so fast there isn't time to do it after dosing the dog! This remedy does not apply after a period of some considerable time has passed, such as a day; it is only for use the instant the wrong substance has been swallowed.

DIET

I have touched on the subject of food elsewhere but there are just a couple of generalities to observe. In the main, Gordons do not respond well to any of the very high protein complete foods. It has been my experience that the lower the protein, always provided that the protein is of good quality, then the better the Gordon fares. High protein content can lead to poor and irritable skin conditions, which bear a resemblance to eczema. There have been instances in the UK of over-excitability and sharp temperament; sometimes the Gordons have been almost hyper-active, due to food. It has been noticed that there have been considerable changes for the better when the protein content in the food has been reduced. In some cases, where the temperament had become quite dangerous, veterinary tests have shown the animal to be over-proteinised and changes in diet certainly brought about the desired effects. The number of feeds per day is entirely up to the owner. I personally prefer to feed twice a day.

It goes without saying that every dog should have constant access to fresh, clean water at all times of the day.

Chapter Eleven

THE GORDON IN BRITAIN

RESTRICTIONS OF WAR

There is no doubt that World War II was responsible for the gene pool which exists in the UK now. This also applies to the Continent. Anyone who did not experience this part of British history will find it difficult to fully understand the implications of trying to find ways to survive a war.

The threat of invasion by the German armies was so great that strict rationing of food was the first priority, as grain was imported, along with many other food substances, from abroad, including America. The long journeys made across the Atlantic were liable to become quite perilous, and history shows that they did. To qualify for a ration of meal for a dog meant proving that the dog was used for work. Farmers' sheep dogs were allowed rations without exception, but gundogs were a luxury, bred to accompany gentlemen on a day's sport. These definitely were denied a food allowance. The outlook was so bleak that the whole of the Dalnagler kennel was destroyed at the outbreak of the war. Many of the wealthy businessmen who were the owners of some of the larger kennels sent stock to America and elsewhere, to be kept safe and so keep the breed alive.

The numbers of Gordons in Britain at the end of the war were very depleted and, although some very caring people had held on to one or two Gordons, often supplementing their dog's food from their own, no-one had ever dared to breed. It would have been impossible to feed an entire litter and if one did – who would buy the pups?

Once the war was over, there was not an immediate return to normal life, and some foods were rationed right up to 1955. By this time there were just a few Gordons produced from what was by now elderly stock, the war having lasted for some six years.

REPLENISHING THE STOCK

Freidal Van Dam came to the UK from Holland in 1946 and brought with her two Gordons, Palmer of the Speygrounds, who was born in 1947 and Maid Marion of Petersfield. These two brought with them new genes, and Mrs Van Dam did breed quite extensively for a great many years, building a very valuable kennel.

Not much importing was done at the end of the war because, although the quarantine period was just three months, there was little money to fund the purchase of stock together with the cost of travel, transport and quarantine, as attention would have turned towards America.

However, Geoff and Alicia Coupe did import two bitches on two separate occasions from Australia, but by this time quarantine had been lengthened to six months. Many breeders who had the money to import declined to do so because of the length of time the dog would be detained. The first bitch Geoff and Alicia brought in was Doonbrae Moyola Lass. Mated to Sh. Ch. Carelanrig Adonis, she only produced one puppy, Timadon Black Knight, who was not shown extensively. However, his mother did exceptionally well and gained her UK title almost as soon as she came out of quarantine. The second bitch, Glenlochay Kilty Rose of Eireannmada, was only shown once before she was retired to maternal duties. Mated to Adonis she produced Sh. Ch. Timadon Brigadoon in 1980. Later, when mated to Ch. Swanley Strathfinella, she produced a litter from which came three Champions – Bramble and Bilberry, bitches, and Briar, a male, who has been used extensively at stud and whose progeny have accounted well for themselves.

There was, for a short time, a dog from South Africa but he was never used at stud. Dr M. Thompson, who was renowned for the Invercassley kennel, was responsible for the import from Norway of Ulvatnets Truls III, but he was a field dog, small in stature and very dark in his colouring, though I believe he had very good hips. Later, Dr Thompson imported a male from Norman Sorby of America. With so little added to the gene pool over the past decade, it is thanks to the careful thinking of today's breeders that Gordons have progressed so far that the UK exports the breed to all parts of the world.

THE LEADING KENNELS

BOYERS
This is the only existing dual-purpose kennel in the UK. Previously the Swanley kennel was the other one but, since Jeannette Allan's death, no dogs have been trained for the field there.

The Boyers kennel 1982: The foundation bitch, Ch. Sikh of Boyers is pictured on the right hand side. Boyers Seil (pictured as a puppy) is on the left.

Bert and Mary Dyde.

The Boyers kennel 1989: Pictured left to right are Boyers Syce (twenty months), Ch. Singh (five years), Ch. Sanna (seven years) Sh. Ch. Seil (nine years), and Ch. Switha (eleven years).

Bert and Mary Dyde.

Ch. Boyers Sanna: On point on a grouse moor.

The Boyers prefix belongs to Jean Osborn. It was granted in 1936, but to promote another breed. Gordons were introduced here in 1972 by the purchase of a bitch who eventually gained her title and was then Ch. Sikh of Boyers. As she gained her show title so she went to Jeannette Allan to be trained for her Working Gundog Certificate, in which she was successful, and therefore became a Champion instead of Show Champion.

Since that time, Mrs Osborn's daughter has taken over the training and handling of the dogs, both in the field and in the show ring. There has followed a list of five Champions, all but one gaining a Working Gundog Certificate, and all go back in direct line to the foundation bitch.

CAREK

This is the prefix of Yvonne Horrocks, who started with Irish Setters but then took on a Gordon pup in 1974. The puppy's name was Cuprea Black Velvet, purchased from a family by the name of Fanning just before they emigrated to Canada. Velvet was to be Yvonne's foundation bitch and, although she was not fond of the show ring, she produced a bitch, Sh. Ch. Carek Blue Angel, who went on to breed four Champions. The most notable of these was Sh. Ch. Carek Bronze Clansman. This dog holds the show winning record for Gordons in the UK, accounting for thirty-two Challenge Certificates, and was the winner of four Gundog Groups as well as a Champion stake (Pedigree Chum). All of these feats had never been done by any Gordon Setter before. Although he won so well, he only produced one Champion son, Slippen Thor, who was only used once at stud.

Sh. Ch. Carek Bronze Clansman: British breed record holder with a total of thirty-two CCs. Owned and handled by Maureen Hart.

Sh. Ch. Carek Ebony Tusker: Top Gordon Setter 1994. Handled by Derek Horrocks.

Bert and Mary Dyde.

Other notable winners are Sh. Ch. Carek Grey Badger and his litter-mate Grey Dove. This pair were sired by Sh. Ch. Dudmoor Mylton of Lourdace. Top Gordon for 1994 is also from this kennel, Sh. Ch. Carek Ebony Tusker: sired by Sh. Ch. Lourdace Mineer of Liric, his dam is Wickenberry Magnolia at Carek. His winnings, which brought him to the top in 1994 are seven CCs (bringing his total to twelve) and Reserve Best in Show at the Setter and Pointer Championship Show.

CARORAE

Carol Laurie applied for this prefix when she realised that her interest in Gordon Setters was liable to be permanent. Her mother had owned Gordons before – in fact the first Gordon that Carol saw was her mother's Dellfort Sweetness, bred by Mrs Simmonds. It was in 1970 that the kennel really came into being, with the purchase of Tess of Everard and, later, William of Everard, both bred by Mr Papworth. Both obtained their show titles, as did their sire Sh. Ch. Yeoman of Cairlie.

Several Caroraes went to become foundation stock to other kennels, including Carorae the Cavalier, who went to Holland and obtained a Dutch Champion title. There are many champions from this kennel but the culmination of Carol's success was when her Sh. Ch. Carorae Dark Princess took the bitch CC at Cruft's in 1982.

Carol also owned Sh. Ch. Wayfarer of Carorae, who was responsible for much of the good stock around in the 1980s. These include Sh. Ch. Carorae the Laird, owned and campaigned to his title by Martin Bayley, and Sh. Ch. Carorae Luscious Lesley, who was owned and campaigned to her title by Barbara Crosbie, who herself has bred some useful stock from this

Sh. Ch. Lourdace Mineer of Liric: Winner of five CCs and seven Reserve CCs. His progeny has accounted for a total of forty-two CCs to date. He is pictured winning the Contest of Champions, handled by his owner, Maureen Justice.

Bert and Mary Dyde.

Mineer to his title, and Sh. Ch. Wickenberry Philosopher at Liric, bred by Jean Quinn. Maureen has bred two Champions by way of Liric Wild Cherry and Liric High Society.

At a 'Contest of Champions' hosted by the Gordon Setter Association, Maureen successfully handled Sh. Ch. Lourdace Mineer of Liric to win the event.

LOURDACE

This is my own prefix. I first sighted Gordon Setters in 1972, but realised that there was more knowledge I needed to acquire before any purchase could be made. I also discovered that there were not many puppies available, so that slowed the purchase process down anyway. Eventually, in 1975, I bought a bitch named Gaelsett Zephyr and, although she was the discarded choice of her litter, this bitch was to be the greater winner. She had her title before the age of three and was Top Gordon Bitch for two years. Sadly, she only ever produced one live puppy, a male, called Lourdace Marcus, who proved his worth in the show ring, but was retired when his owners started a family of their own. He was, however, used at stud and it is his progeny that are still making their mark.

Next came another bitch named Winterwood Moonbeam who, although she only ever whelped one litter, to Ch. Swanley Strathbeg, was to be the foundation of my kennel. Moonbeam was trained by me and ran in trials for two seasons. From the only litter she had came two Show Champions. One, a male, gained his title and was then sold to Holland where

Sh. Ch. Winterwood Moonbean (pictured at eleven years of age): Foundation bitch for the Lourdace kennel.

Bert and Mary Dyde.

he did well, producing some nice pups for his new owners, until he was put to sleep at the age of thirteen years. Hank and Wil Huizer were his Dutch owners; his name was Sh. Ch. Lourdace Spectrum.

The bitch from this mating was Lourdace Silica. From matings with Sh. Ch. Dudmoor Mylton of Lourdace she produced Sh. Ch. Lourdace Mink, Sh. Ch. Lourdace Mystique and Lourdace Tamarisk who, sold to Monsieur Barnili in France and passed on to M. Dennis, in 1986 was declared European Champion. Silica, mated to Rossend Gaelic Storm, produced a litter from which came Sh. Ch. Lourdace Graph Spae. This bitch, in turn, gave birth to her first litter by Sh. Ch. Gladstone of Lourdace, producing eight pups, of which three were liver and tan in colour. From the remaining black and tans came two Show Champions named Lourdace Gandolf (male) and Grimalkin (bitch). From Graph Spae's last litter, which was the result of an alliance with Northinch Briar of Keepersgate, came five whelps, three of whom are Champions. These include Lourdace Bronco and Black Rose, who are in Switzerland, and Bridoon who is owned by me.

Bought in as a pup came Sh. Ch. Dudmoor Mylton of Lourdace. He was a very prolific

*Sh. Ch. Lourdace
Gandolf of
Amanorty, handled
by Kath Howard.*

stud, siring eight Champions, many of whom may still get their titles. He took the national award of Top Sire on eight consecutive occasions and has had a vast effect on the breed, all of it good. Peggy Grayson, a well-known International judge, was so impressed with him she made him Best in Show.

Sh. Ch. Gladstone of Lourdace is a double grandson of Mylton, coming from a half-brother to half-sister mating. This male was awarded Best in Show at Breed shows four times. He won a total of twenty-seven Challenge Certificates and was top winning Gordon for 1987 and 1988. In Ireland he was awarded two Green Stars. I had hoped to break the CC record with him but, sadly, ill health overtook him and he was retired from the ring, but he continues to sire excellent stock. Northinch Briar was purchased at the age of two and is also a very prolific sire. He was Top Sire in 1992 and 1993. It is his son, Sh. Ch. Lourdace Buccaneer of Benbreac, who graces the cover of this book.

When the Gordon Setter Association hosted a 'Contest of Champions' in 1990, Lourdace fielded eight contestants and the eventual winner was Sh. Ch. Lourdace Minner of Liric, the result of a mating between Sh. Ch. Lourdace Mink and Winterwood Summercloud. From a mating to Sh. Ch. Timadon Brigadoon, Summercloud produced Lourdace Bullion who won almost everything that there was to win for his owners in Switzerland, Erwin and Heidi Karrer. He did become World Champion, but, sadly, he died in his sleep at the age of six. A post mortem revealed that he had lung cancer. To date, Lourdace has produced sixteen Champions.

Ch. Swanley Strathbeg: Best in Show at the Setter and Pointer Championship Show 1978.

Swanley Strathtuath: Trained by Jeanette Allan and run in trials by 'Pop' Allan. This bitch won in the field in 1986 and 1987.

SWANLEY

When I came into Gordons in 1975, this kennel had been established for some thirty years. It was founded by the late Jeanette Allan, who started the line with this prefix under the name of Hall. The line is now in the capable hands of her daughter Alison Allan.

Jeanette had been a great sportswoman, one of her favourite activities being fishing, although her real interest was in working Gordon Setters. However, this was not the only breed that she owned and bred. There have been some very useful Pointers and Labradors, who were also kept as working gundogs to accompany Jeanette and 'Pop', as George Allan was affectionately known, on any shooting expeditions.

Jeanette was a great believer in the dual-purpose Gordon and always strove to inspire others to work their Gordons, whether they were bred for show or field or simply purchased as a pet. She loved the Scottish moors and was lucky enough to be able to spend all of her life close to the moors or, with some keeper's permission, to use them for training. She personally trained her Gordons, although in her latter years this became increasingly more difficult due to a horrendous car accident which left her with such damage to her legs that surgeons told her she would never walk again. However, not surprisingly, Jeanette defied them all and learned to walk all over again. The moorland, with its rough and uneven terrain, was most difficult, yet she persisted. I consider myself fortunate to have been able to stay with Jeanette and to become a pupil for a short while so that I witnessed the wonderful control she had, with even the rawest of novices. It is no mean feat to venture on to a rugged moor with a walking stick in each hand, one of which held a check cord with a young Gordon on the end. Her control with her soft voice had to be seen to be fully understood.

All the Gordons retained by this kennel gained their Working Gundog Certificates, or won awards in the field to allow them to attain the title of Champion, rather than Show Champion. The first one that I became acquainted with was Ch. Swanley Strathbeg. He was Top Gordon nationally during the years 1978 and 1979. His mother, Ch. Swanley Strathspey, had won in the field as well as on the bench. Sadly his demise came at only six years of age, struck down by cancer. His winnings were indeed impressive: twenty-one Challenge Certificates, most accompanied by Best of Breed awards, and Best in Show at the Setter & Pointer Championship Show in 1978. A winner at Crufts in 1980, he was included in the Group final six for further consideration. Strathbeg was also Best in Show at Tay Valley Gundog Show and Reserve Best in Show at Gundog Breeds of Scotland Championship Show. There was a brother, not a littermate but bred the same way, named Swanley Strathfinella. This dog accounted well for himself in the ring and also achieved his Working Gundog Certificate. He was also a Group winner at the Scottish Kennel Club's show and, at the age of almost nine years, was the winner of a large entry for the Veteran Stakes (All Gundogs).

Another top winner was Ch. Swanley Strathalmuree. This bitch, mated to Lourdace Sebastian, a son of Strathbeg, produced a lovely litter from which Swanley Strathtuath was retained. This bitch was to win in the field before she even saw a show ring. Born in 1984, she was winning in the field in 1986 and 1987. Some of these trials have special Trophies and Strathtuath won the Invercassley Trophy for the best display of quartering and handling the ground. She took this from an entry of seventy-five dogs. Her second prestigous win was to be awarded the Astor Trophy for the best Setter. This had never been won by a Gordon before.

Alison has only had control for a short while but in that time she has bred two very successful litters who, due to their tender years, have yet to achieve great heights.

WALLBANK

This affix is owned by Ric and Jill Dixon and was granted to them in 1986, although their interest commenced in 1982 when they purchased their first Gordon, a bitch named Majestic Doe. Bought solely to be a pet, her sire was Lourdace Marcus and her dam Tripoint Big Girl. Big Girl's pedigree was mostly working stock. Bo, as Majestic Doe was known to her friends, died tragically in 1990 after an unsuccessful operation, but not before she had produced a litter after a mating with Sh. Ch. Carek Grey Badger. This was a line bred litter,

Sh. Ch. Wallbank Black Bryony (Sh. Ch. Carek Grey Badger – Majestic Doe). Owned by Ric and Jill Dixon.

as Lourdace Marcus was sired by Sh. Ch. Dudmoor Mylton of Lourdace the same sire as Sh. Ch. Carek Grey Badger, half-brother to half-sister in fact.

From the mating a dog and a bitch were retained. These were Wallbank Black Bryony and Wallbank Bittersweet. Another sibling Bluebell was sold on to become foundation bitch to Lyn and Chris Davies (Shehallion). The male, Black Bryony, was top puppy in 1986, gained his title in 1989 and finished the year as Top Winning Gordon male, accounting for seven CCs, six Best of Breeds, and six Reserve CCs. Bluebell also gained her title, and thus two Show Champions came from this first litter.

Wallbank Bittersweet, although not campaigned to her title, came into her own as a brood bitch. Mated to Sh. Ch. Gladstone of Lourdace, who was himself a double grandson of 'Mylton', she produced a litter in October 1988. From this mating came two exceptional bitches – W. Sweet Success and W. Sweet Sensation. Sh. Ch. Wallbank Sweet Success started her career by being made Best Puppy in Show at the Gordon Setter Association Championship Show 1989, and then was quickly made to Show Champion in the capable hands of her owner Angeler Backler. Sweet Success has become the foundation bitch of the Kalinish kennel. The other bitch, Sweet Sensation, was never really campaigned, but mated to Wallbank Kalinish Success Story, she produced a litter from which Ric and Jill have kept a bitch puppy – Wallbank Joie de Vivre.

Sweet Success's first litter was to Sh. Ch. Wallbank Black Bryony, and from this litter Ric and Jill took a male – Wallbank Kalinish Success Story. Wallbank Bittersweet had a second litter in 1990. She was mated by her son from the first litter and it was an unplanned liaison. Ric and Jill kept a bitch, Wallbank Sporting Luck, who is being campaigned currently.

The ambition of this small kennel is to follow a policy of line breeding, hopefully producing Gordons of consistent quality who reflect the essence of the Breed Standard, with particular reference to type, size, correct colour (eyes and coat), temperament and soundness.

FIELD TRIALLING

ASSARTS

Bob Truman, holder of the Assarts prefix, is probably, along with George Burgess, one of the most renowned men on the Field Trial scene today.

He was first introduced to Gordon Setters in 1943 when he was looking through a National Geographical Magazine where there was an article which discussed the merits of four bird dogs. This was accompanied by a coloured picture depicting a Gordon Setter. The black and tan colouring of the Gordon made a lasting impression and, even at the relatively tender age that he was then, Bob became hooked for life. Yet it was to be another five years before he renewed that first acquaintance.

He decided to take regular delivery of the Gamekeeper and Countryside magazine and, one day, there appeared a brief advertisement offering Gordon Setter pups for sale in Scotland. Although Bob does not remember the locality exactly, he does remember quite clearly that an eight-week-old pup cost him five guineas, which included delivery, something which made a great impression on him as this figure represented exactly half of one week's wages in those days. Sadly, no pedigree was forthcoming, and neither was the registration.

The pup was sent down by train, which was met by Bob, who was indeed very excited as he enquired at the ticket office if his delivery had been made. The reply was: "He's in the signal box." Bob remembers dashing up the steps to the signal box two at a time, so eager was he to catch sight of his purchase. The pup was there alright, tied with twine to one of the long rank of huge gleaming signal levers, while the signalman tossed portions of his sandwiches to him, who caught them very adeptly. The operation of the railways was relatively unpretentious in those days and the telegraph bell tinged twice, imperiously advertising the arrival of the five-fifteen on the up line. Bob didn't hear it, he was so in love with this bundle, and has remained so ever since.

Bob spent a lot of time out in South Africa, returning to the UK in 1962. He discovered that working Gordons were extremely thin on the ground so, in spite of feeling like a traitor, he took up with a show-bred English Setter, Withinlee Winston by name. Bob campaigned him with some success in the show ring and liked the dog very much, later breeding him to Sh.Ch. Fenman Fragrance, but he still aspired to the working setters. One day he attended a Field demonstration under the able command of Auriol Mason who, together with her Irish Acornbank Setters, gave some convincing display of essentials, including the sound advice: "What is required is a grand going dog, full of style, pace and enthusiasm." Bob has always tried to keep that axiom at the forefront of his dog-working endeavours.

What with one thing and another, Bob did not actually get to spectate at a field trial until 1970, when he drove up overnight to Slaggyford in Cumbria. Here he learned, and digested, some of the basics of trialling, helped immensely by a long and instructive talk by the late Col. Sydney Balding MC. He was allowed to hold Dr Maurice's dogs and watched the Gordon Setters, Crafnant Teal and Clitters Katy Gordon, at work; he admired the Headkeeper, David Parkinson's quiet and efficient management of the trial and sought to find the secrets lurking behind the competence of such handlers as George Burgess, Tom Spark, Tom Lauder and Bertie McElhinney.

Field Trial Ch. Assarts Acorn of Carrissa, owned by Mike Daw.

Bob remembers the late Dr Michael Good asking him, when they were outside the Hillcrest Hotel in Alston: "Ah, where are you staying?" to which Bob replied: "Oh, I have a little place down the road." In fact, for economic reasons, he had catnapped in the back of his car with his feet hanging out of the window, waking later only to find that it had rained all night and his legs and feet were absolutely sodden. "You must show me where it is," exclaimed the Doctor. "Bound to be cheaper than this place!"

He exchanged pleasantries with George Burgess in the hotel car park after the first day of the trial. George was muttering to himself as he fed his dog, Dodger, in the back of his van. There had been some kind of a contretemps during the running of the second round. George was cussing his dog, although he was giving him extra food as a treat. Bob remarked that he thought he was out of favour, only to have George quickly say "But he came back, didn't he?" Bob decided that this was the man from whom to learn about Gordons.

A second Gordon did not take up residence with Bob until the following year, when he deemed himself lucky to be able to purchase Freebirch Farmer, who was to be the first of several dogs from Barbara Swindon, in Derbyshire. The advert did say 'not show': this dog had a white toe and a large splash of white down his chest, rather like the painting of Gordons done so very many years ago. However, Bob felt that he looked right for him and so the sale was completed. This dog was worked on very hard, for Bob was determined to have proper control and was anxious to avoid any risk of being found wanting under the searching eyes of the experts, or of being awed by any real or imagined hint of jealousy possibly, and unconsciously, emanating from experienced participants. This is an integral part of any firing and tempering process, and the essential catalyst in eventual competence, a factor not always appreciated by today's newcomer handler.

Bob read and re-read the authoritative writings of Arkwright, Marr, Hutchinson, Maurice and Moxon; and after trudging many miles, in all weathers, with the aid of whistles, check cords and the countless expending of .22 blanks, he finally entered for a Novice Stake.

Competing in that stake was not to be, for 1972 found Bob back in Africa, complete with Gordon Setter, where he discovered very active Field Trial Clubs in both Rhodesia (as it was then) and in South Africa. The main quarry birds were several species of Francolin, Guinea fowl, and Quail. All buck and fur are treated as game and must be pointed.

Because the high veldt is covered with quite tall grass and scrub trees, dogs must vary the width of the beat according to the thickness of cover, in order to maintain visible contact with the handler; and, with poor scenting conditions, birds are invariably pointed when right on the end of the dog's nose. Heat factors dictate that trials start around 6 a.m., with a midday break of several hours, until things cool again. European goosegrass and cockleburr are as nothing compared with the diabolically conceived, surgically hooked, barbed grass and foliage that this Continent can offer – ticks of all sizes abound and the attendant risk of stepping on a comatose snake was constantly present. Since there were no keepers, the handler carried the gun.

Bob purchased two more Gordons and had them sent to him in Rhodesia. They were, Invercassley Jock Scott and Freebirch Fortune. These two completed a team, not just of Gordon Setters but of winning Gordons in the field trial scene in Rhodesia and South Africa, scoring in the Champion Stakes in both countries.

1978 saw Bob returning to England, dogs in quarantine, but still undaunted. Within three weeks of coming out of confinement, they were in the trials awards again. This was the year that Bob acquired the famous tricoloured Gordon from Barbara Swindon – his name, Freebirch Vincent. To all intents and purposes, Bob claims, he stole him from Barbara! That year Bob registered his affix – Assarts. He got the word from history, learning that King Henry II, in order to clear high Oxfordshire of forest, granted what was called an Assart to whoever felled and stumped a prescribed area. That person could then possess the cleared land. The farmhouse Bob lived in at that time was linked to its four hundred year old past by its name – Glympton Assarts.

All Bob's dogs who have gained success have run solely under their breeder's kennel prefix, if only to do no more than recognise and acknowledge the large part that Freebirch, Invercassley and Cairnlora kennels have played in his many achievements.

A further pup from Barbara Swindon, Freebirch Viner, was procured the following year and both he and Vincent, together with Invercassley Jock Scott, gained their titles (Field Trial Champion).

In 1980, Cairnlora Black Domino arrived to join the Assarts kennel. She was in lieu of a stud fee and went on to become a brood bitch, after some very good wins. Bob campaigned all his dogs steadily and with much enjoyment and gratification, thus establishing a proven breeding nucleus, and four years later a homebred bitch was trialled, Assarts Baroness. Following on came Dr Beasley's Assarts Ambrose, Bob's own Assarts Actress, Mike Daw's FT Ch. Assarts Acorn of Carrissa, Katherine Settry's Assarts Black Tarn and Assarts Silva Barron, who in the USA is Adam Wilson Young's FT Ch. Assarts Lorne, Dr. Thompson's Assarts Wild Alice, Bob's FT Ch. Assarts Scorcher and Assarts Krispin, who is trained and trialled by Bob's wife Gill; all are award winners.

A gift from Spain gave Bob another winner in Altzaga Blacksmith of Assarts. He went on to produce Gawett (second affix to Assarts) Aviator who was an award winner in 1993.

Bob shoots over his dogs on a regular basis, which he considers to be important. It was something he did both in South Africa and here in England. It confirms that dogs used in competition can be capable of a hard day's work on the hill. Bob has imported a stud dog, whose progeny were already winning, from Jarle Johansen in Norway. This was a decision that Bob took to provide a boost to the currently restricted working gene pool, as it was causing him some concern.

This is what having Gordons is all about – keeping an eye on the future. Bob Truman is an eminent man in his field; he has a rapport with any dog he comes across. His record of success says it all. He has always been willing to help anyone who asks and has devoted much of his spare time to teaching others, such as the members of Setter and Pointer Clubs, to understand what training is all about. He has written a book to assist anyone who is interested in learning, proving what an unselfish man he is.

COMPETITIVE OBEDIENCE

Barbara Riste is probably the only person who is competing in Championship Obedience Competitions with Gordon Setters. She is the proud owner of three Gordons, and has done all the vast training herself. Barbara first encountered the breed when she attended Crufts Dog Show some years ago. She came across a male Gordon who was sitting on his bench, protesting loudly at being left. For Barbara it was love at first sight. At this point she became determined to find out more about the breed, and was soon confident that she and Gordons would be compatible.

Barbara's first acquisition was a bitch purchased from Karen May and registered as Gemwell Lady of the Lake. By 1983 Lady of the Lake had earned the titles – CDEX, UDEX and WDX. In 1988 the young bitch that Barbara had bought to follow on from Lady of the Lake, namely Gemwell Poetry in Motion, joined the family. Poetry in Motion also accounted well for herself and earned the titles CDEX, UDEX and WDEX.

Having achieved almost as many titles as are available to her, Barbara has quite recently taken on another youngster from the same kennel, namely Gemwell Black Grouse. Barbara

Gemwell Lady of the Lake CD Ex, UD Ex, WD Ex.

Gemwell Lady of the Lake in action going over the 6ft scale.

has always been helped with an insight into the breed by the breeder of her three Gordons and this relationship should surely exist with every owner and their breeder. Sadly this is not always the case.

WORKING TITLES
Titles to be attained in the UK are: CD = Companion Dog; UD = Utility Dog; WD = Working Dog; TD = Tracking Dog and PD = Patrol Dog. CD is the lowest of these awards and very much Obedience orientated, with a search square included in the test but without any tracking. Utility Dog Stake is divided into three groups. Group 1 is marked as follows:

Group 1	Marks
1. Heel Free	5
2. Sending Dog Away	10
3. Retrieving Dumbell	5
4. Down 10 mins out of sight	10
5. Steadiness to Gunshot	5

Total: 35   Minimum Qualifying Mark: 25

Group 2	Agility	Marks
6. Clear Jump		5
7.Long Jump		5
8. Scale (3) Stay (2) Recall (5)		10

Total: 20   Minimum Qualifying Mark: 14

Group 3	Nosework	Marks
Search		35
Track (95) Article(15)		110

Total: 145   Minimum Qualifying Mark: 102

Grand total: 200   Minimum Qualifying Mark: 141

For PD and WD, it is necessary to track a ninety minute old trail and find two articles. For TD it is necessary to track a three hour old trail with three articles involved. In PD, manwork is also required.The track is laid by a tracklayer walking to a pattern provided by the judge and turning as instructed. The higher the Stake the more turns are made. Scented articles are left on the track and it is the scent left behind by the tracklayer that the dog must follow.

Chapter Twelve

THE GORDON IN NORTH AMERICA

EARLY HISTORY

The first documentation concerning Gordon Setters in America comes from an official importation order, relating to dogs from Gordon Castle, allowing them to enter America. This application was made by a man called George Blunt, in 1842, and the document refers to dogs named Rake and Rachel. It may well have been that these dogs were tri-coloured, as a painting, drawn by an artist by the name of Pope, shows Rake as a white dog with a black saddle marking, although there is mention of tan markings as well. It also is written that Rake had a very curly coat. Rachel was given to Daniel Webster, the American statesman and orator. The Blunts and Websters apparently raised hunting dogs from this original pair until after the turn of the century.

The earliest registration, however, was made in 1879 by one J. White, who registered a dog named Bang with the National American Kennel Club, which subsequently merged into what is now known as the American Kennel Club. Bang was whelped in December 1975. He was by the imported Shot out of White's Nell.

In the latter part of the nineteenth century a great sporting gentleman, named Henry Malcolm, bred many Black and Tan Setters at his large kennel in Maryland. He used his dogs strictly for hunting, but he also became involved with the development of the breed. He was responsible for the formation of Gordon Setter breed clubs, and in 1891 the first Standard of the breed was produced, based largely on Malcolm's work.

Dog shows began in the United States in the mid-1870s. In 1877 the first Westminster Kennel Club Show was held in New York City. This was a three day show with an entry of 1194, which included an entry of seventy-nine Gordon Setters, both native and imported. The importation of Gordons from Great Britain reached a peak during the late 1800s. During this period such imports as Grouse, Bee, Blossom, Beaumont, Bellmont, Heather Bee, Heather Roy, Heather Lad and Duke of Edgeworth did consistent winning at dog shows, and in those days it was very difficult for the native Gordon Setter to win against such strong British opposition. In 1892 the American Kennel Club officially changed the name of the breed from Black and Tan Setter to Gordon Setter. This was twenty-five years before the British Kennel Club made the same change.

The first recorded Field Trial took place in 1874 in Memphis, Tennessee. Nearly all the entries were listed as "Setters". The Gordon Setter Club, formed by Harry Malcolm, held trials in 1893 and 1894. These were reported to have been poorly supported and were not continued. A growing campaign aimed at conserving rapidly vanishing game bird species, coupled with a change in the hunting style of Americans, caused a dramatic decline in the popularity of Gordons in America.

By the early 1900s, only a handful of Gordons were exhibited at the Westminster Kennel Club show and most of the Gordon breeding kennels were closed. In the period from 1910 to 1920 there was little dog show activity for Gordon Setters, and the First World War further reduced the dog population in North America.

THE GORDON REVIVAL

Around 1920, Charles T. Inglee set about reviving the Gordon Setter in America. Mr Inglee was unable to find enough stock in America, though he did made good use of a male he discovered on Long Island, New York. This dog was called Governor Edwards (imported Stylish Ben out of American & Canadian Champion Trampus Shannon), and he became Mr Inglee's first Show Champion.

Unfortunately, the British Gordon Setter was also in decline following the First World War, and so Mr Inglee turned his attention to Scandinavia, where Gordons were a blending of British and Scandinavian bloodlines. Mr Inglee's kennel was called Inglehurst, and the first import to carry the Inglehurst name was Joker, whelped in 1920. A successful show dog, Joker also had great success as a sire, producing seventy-eight litters (over three hundred puppies), twenty of whom became Show Champions. Nine of these were the result of matings to Ch. Petra. By 1935, Mr Inglee had produced three hundred Gordon litters and a total of forty Show Champions.

Active not only in breeding and showing, Mr Inglee organised the new Gordon Setter Club of America in 1924. This club soon became a member of the American Kennel Club, and it is the organization in the United States under which most Gordon Setter Specialties (an all-Gordon Conformation show), Field Trials and Hunting Tests (a relatively new test of dogs' hunting abilities) are run. There are also two licensed Gordon clubs in the United States, both in the Eastern US Current membership in the Gordon Setter Club of American stands at over one thousand members. The TarTan Gordon Setter Club has more than one hundred and fifty members from throughout the New England area, and it runs Field Trials, Specialties and Hunting Tests under its own banner, as does the smaller Paumanauk Gordon Setter Club, which draws its membership from the Long Island, New York area. Of more recent origin is the Gordon Setter Club of Canada.

INFLUENTIAL KENNELS

Inglehurst dogs continued to influence the development of the American Gordon Setter long after Mr Inglee ceased to breed them himself. They were behind many important kennels of the early to mid-1900s, including the Svane kennels of Dr A.P. Evans; Dr Rixford's kennel in California, and other Californian kennels operated by John Taafe and Alec Laurence, as well as Donald Fordyce's Clonmellerslie Gordons. Mr Fordyce was a founding member of the "new" Gordon Setter Club of America along with Mr Inglee, and he served for many years as the Secretary of the American Kennel Club. Inglehurst dogs are also found as

Dual Ch. Gordon Hill Chantilly Lace: A national Specialty BOS winner, who produced two Dual Champions among her six Champion offspring. The Gordon Hill kennel has been active since the 1940s.

important contributors to the Thistlerock kennel of William Cary Duncan, the Gregorach kennel of James Munn (who figure prominently in the Windy Hills kennel of Jake and Dottie Poisker), and the Marcella kennel of James Powell and Rank Morgan.

In the 1930s Charles and Edna Giradot began breeding Gordons at their kennel in Scotia, New York. They used both "EEG" and "Scotia" as kennel names, sometimes the two in combination. Mrs Giradot traced the pedigree of her first Champion bitch, Ch. Larrabee's Avalon Beauty, back to the Gordon Castle strain. This huge undertaking was published in the *Gordon Setter Club of America Yearbook in 1939*. This book was published by the Gordon Setter Club of America, the first of its kind. There was not to be another until 1963. This was followed by three more yearbooks, the last being published in 1977. The club followed the

Ch. Afternod Sybilla: The Afternod Gordon Setters have had a great influence on the development of the breed in North America. This bitch was the foundation for the Stillmeadows kennel.

yearbook with another hardback publication, entitled *The Gordon Setter Review 1978-1988*, which chronicled the achievements for Gordons during that decade. The GSCA also publishes a monthly newsletter (500th issue: Fall 1994), a yearly Pictorial, which contains photographs and pedigrees of current Gordons, as well as many, many regional newsletters by local area committees and by the two other independent Gordon clubs, TarTan and Paumanauk.

Dr Claude Searle of Chicago's Serlway kennel began his involvement with Gordons about 1936. He imported two British Gordons, Downside Bonnie of Serlway and Valiant Nutmeg of Serlway which produced well. Nutmeg produced twelve Show Champions – quite an achievement for a dam. Bonnie had an exciting show career and was shown by Dick Cooper of Illinois, still an active handler in the 1990s!

Important kennels in the 1930s and 40s included Blakeen, owned by Mrs Sherman Hoyt and founded on British imports. (These dogs became the foundation stock of the Loch Ridge kennel of George Thompson of Baltimore, Maryland.); Heslop, operated by George and Myrtle Heslop, Jonesville, New York, whose Ch. Heslop's Courageous is behind most of the Bench and field Gordon Champions in the US today.

Like the First World War, the Second World War also had a devastating impact on the breeding and exhibiting of all pedigree dogs in the US – Gordons included. As a result, the period from the mid-1940s to the close of the decade was a quiet one. Registrations began to pick up again in 1949, and a number of influential kennels emerged. These included: Newcomers, Thurston's (also known as Thor's Hill), Halenfred, Sun-Yak (still in operation in the state of Washington today), Windy Hill, Gordon Hill (another kennel still active today), Sangerfield and Loch Adair. The Afternod kennel of Marion Wilcox of Connecticut was registered in 1946 and has had a major impact on the breed in the last half of the 20th century.

Gordon activities in both the United States and Canada have continued to expand. The recently formed Gordon Setter Club of Canada has held four National Specialties to date. Annually the Gordon Setter Club of Americ multi-purpose dog. The Gordon Setter Club of America has recognised the breed's versatility by designating dogs achieving titles in Obedience, Conformation and Field competition as "Beauty, Brains and Birdsense" award winners, which is a coveted honour. It has to be said that nowhere in the world is the Gordon so versatile as it is in America, where the same animal can become involved with so many activities open to the canine community. Although there are kennels which breed solely for the purpose of work, and at least one which boasts that it breeds to order, it is mainly the show-bred animal which proves that nothing is impossible for the Gordon Setter. Trained for Obedience, show ring, work as a rough shooter, Agility, Fly-ball, and Field Trialling, this versatility endears the Gordon even more as a pet and valued companion.

MODERN GORDON KENNELS

ALILOU

Owned by Louise Rosskamp & L. Alison Rosskamp, Pennsylvania. This kennel has bred Gordon Setters since the 1970s, and is the home of multiple Specialty winners, Obedience-

FIELD TRIALLING IN THE UNITED STATES

A young Gordon on a check cord learning to follow scent.

Learning to stay down when birds are on the wing. One of these has failed!

ABOVE: Gordons waiting patiently for their turn at a training session for field work.

RIGHT: This young bitch has retrieved her prize, a pigeon, and is returning to her handler.

titled and Hunting-titled Gordons. Alison Rosskamp is the co-owner of Ch. Woodsmoke's After Hours, one of a select number of US Best in Show bitches. This kennel has a reputation for owning and/or breeding top producing sires and dams. Some breeding is carried out in association with Colleen O'Brien, Pennsylvania, of the Fair Isle Gordons.

ALISTAIR
Owned by Oliver & Gerald Reimer, Minnesota. This kennel had the distinction of breeding Am. Can. Ch. Alistair's Woodland Gael, No. 1 Bench Gordon 1985, Top Ten Gordon 1984-86. 'Gaelen' was always owner-handled by Ollie and Gerry's son, Kerry, who breeds Gordons under the Kerrymoore prefix. Alistair Gordons have excelled in Bench and Obedience competition.

ARMADALE
Owned by Rick & Deb Klem, Michigan. A relatively new kennel, which has produced Specialty winners in both the US and Canada. Their goal is to produce sound, sensible Gordons.

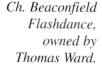

Ch. Beaconfield Flashdance, owned by Thomas Ward.

BEACONFIELD
Owned by Thomas Ward, California. Beaconfield's foundation bitch, Ch. Penchris Eilea Ness McVay, was a top producer with many Specialty winning offspring, whose own offspring continue to win Specialties. Field Champion Beaconfield Captain Fantastic was bred by this kennel.

BELMOR
Joel & Barbara Morris, Virginia. Established in the early 1960s, this kennel has produced

many Field Champions, award winners, and top producing Field sires and dams based on a very limited breeding programme. Among the more notable Gordons from Belmor are: Field Champion Belmors Pretty Belle, 10 times Field Champion (AKC and American Field) Belmors Pretty Missy, Belmors Knight, Belmors Allspice Ginger, Belmors Highland Laddie and MacGeowls Braird. Barbara Morris is the owner of the first AKC Open National Field Champion, Belmor's Knight Train. Joel was a contributing editor to two GSCA Yearbooks, and the 1978-1988 Review.

BERRIDALE
Owned by William & Jeanine Dwelly, South Carolina. Breeders of Gordons since the mid-1970s, this kennel bred the top winning Ch. Laird Duncan of Berridale, and one of the breed's top brood bitches, Ch. Berridale's Sundance Sarah. Bill is the current GSCA delegate to the American Kennel Club, and is also a licensed judge.

BLACK ANVIL
Owned by Phyllis Perelli, Connecticut. Gordons have been bred here since the early 1970s, with the distinction of owning Ch. Gordon Hill Run For Daylight, a Specialty winner, and a top producing sire of over twenty Bench Champions and two dual Champions. This kennel has bred numerous Specialty winners and top producers.

BRAWRIDGE
Owned by Robert Mellis, Pennsylvania. Perhaps Brawridge is best-known for producing the multiple all-breed Best in Show and multiple Specialty winning Am. Can. Ch. Brawridge TNT Of Kris, first Gordon to have been awarded the Quaker Oats Sporting Dog of the Year (1988), winner of some twenty-two Best in Shows. This kennel has also owned or bred numerous other Specialty winning Gordons.

Am. Can. Ch. Brawridge TNT Of Kris: Winner of some twenty-two Best in Show awards. Owned by Robert Mellis.

BRENTWOOD
Owned by Charles & Pam Krothe, Indiana.
This kennel bred the 1993 Breed Gordon Setter of the Year, Ch. Brentwood's Magnum P.I. Relatively new on the Gordon scene, the Brentwood dogs have made an impressive showing in the Specialty ring, capturing many top honours..

BRIGHT STAR
Owned by Matt, Wendy & Tracy Czarnecki, California.
Breeders and/or owners of Gordons successful on the Bench, in the Field and in Obedience competition. They have bred or owned multiple Specialty winners and dogs with Hunting titles. Wendy is an editor of *Gordon Quarterly* magazine.

BROMWICH
Owned by Suzanne & Roy Montgomery, New York.
This kennel breeds English, Irish and Gordon Setters. Gordon Setters joined the strength in the early 1980s, and bred/owned Ch. Bromwich's Full Stride, multiple Specialty winner, including the 1990 National Specialty, and top producing sire. Suzanne Montgomery of the Wildwood Gordon Setters is John and Virginia Radonios's daughter.

BUNNERS
Owned by Linda Bunner, Michigan.
This kennel has bred Show Champions, hunting companions, and family friends, with the emphasis on sound, healthy Gordons with good temperaments.

Ch. Buteo's Firebird: The foundation and top producing sire for the Buteo kennel. Owned by Susan Kilby.

BUTEO
Owned by Susan G. Kilby.
Established in 1979, Susan's foundation bitch, Ch. Pandora's Magdelene of Buteo, produced Ch. Buteo's Firebird, her foundation and top producing sire. Firebird was the sire of Ch. Buteo's Great Miami, the Top Winning Gordon Setter of all times (Breed System), winning Best of Breed at twenty-nine Specialty Shows over a period of seven years, including a National Specialty. He was also a multiple Best in Show winner. His litter brother, Ch. Buteo's Colorado, was also a National Specialty Best of Breed winner. The dam of these boys is Ch. Buteo's Night Owl, Buteo's top producing bitch, with twelve Champions. Buteo's Kennels has produced fifty-three Champions to date, including the latest Specialty winner, Ch. Buteo's Confederate Dream, another Firebird son.

Representatives of the Chaparral kennel: Ch. Chapparal Ace's High CD, MH (left) pictured with Jess, and four of their daughters who all became Champions.

CHAPARRAL
Owned by Linda Sanders, Nevada.
This kennel was established in 1972, and Linda states that she is "dedicated to producing good-looking, good-working Gordons with natural hunting, pointing and retrieving instincts." She breeds for dogs with sound bodies and willing temperaments. As of January 1994, Chaparral has produced forty-three Champions, one Dual Champion, one Field Champion, twenty-eight Companion Dog titlists (CD), three Companion Dog Excellent titlists (CDX), one Utility Dog (UD), thirty-three Junior Hunters, eight Senior Hunters, and four Master Hunters.

CLANMUIR
Owned by Maribeth & Dan McGinty, Nevada. This is a small kennel dedicated to producing "3B" Gordons. Owners of Dual Ch. Chaparral Instant Pride SH.

CLANSMEN
Owned by Jim Stomp. This kennel was stablished early 1970s, and has the distinction of breeding and owning Ch. Clansmen Colourgard, a top producing sire, as well as many other top producers, Group and Specialty winners.

DON-D
Owned by Don & Dottie Selle, New York. Established in 1965, this kennel bred and owned the Specialty winning Ch. Don-D's Citation.

DOUBLEDEE
Owned by Gwynne McDevitt, Pennsylvania. Breeder and/or owner of many GSCA award winners in the Field Trial categories.

DUNBAR
Owned by Jim Thacker, Ohio. Perhaps the most notable dog to be campaigned by this kennel was Dual and Amateur Field Champion Shadowmere Scylla Savoy, bred by Jack & Barbara Cooper of California. Jim was the Chairman of the first GSCA National Specialty in 1983.

FALCONS
Owned by Pat Sanborn & Nils Sanborn, Pennsylvania. Owners and/or breeders of GSCA award winners in the Field Trial categories. Most notable is Field Champion/Amateur Field Champion Falcon's Knight Jenny.

FAUCONNIERS
Owned by Stuart & Julie Burgard, California. Breeders of Specialty winners, Obedience and Hunting titlists. The kennels' owners pledge: "We are committed to breeding sound and healthy Gordons that are capable and worthy of doing it all!"

FEUNOIR
Owned by Ginette & Jacque Babin, Ontario, Canada. Breeder of Am. Can. Ch. Feunoir Autumn Sonata, winner of both the 1991 Canadian National Specialty and American National Specialty (Winners Dog in 1989, and Best of Breed in 1993).

His mother, Am. Can. Ch. Tri-Sett Hit-Parade Feunoir CD, was herself a National Specialty Winners Bitch in 1984, and was top bitch in Canada in 1986. Their daughter, Feunoir Copie Conforme, joined her father in the Specialty winners' circle in 1993 by earning the Winners Bitch award.

FIELDSTONE
Owned by Mary Ann Alston, Maryland. This kennel has Irish Setters, English Cockers and

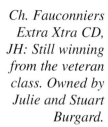

Ch. Fauconniers Extra Xtra CD, JH: Still winning from the veteran class. Owned by Julie and Stuart Burgard.

Gordon Setters, and is responsible for numerous Specialty winners. Mrs Alston is approved to judge all Sporting Breeds.

GAMBIT

Owned by Edward J. Fronczak, Michigan. This kennel specialises in producing "Gordon Setters with a British accent". Originally known for his association with Shojin Gordons, Mr Fronczak established the Gambit kennel several years ago. He has imported Lourdace Dauntless and Lourdace Grand Marnier from the Lourdace kennel, Britain.

GORDON HILL

Owned by Muriel Clement & Susan DeSilver, Connecticut. Gordon Hill was established in 1946 by Mrs Muriel Clement. The hallmark of this small breeding kennel is fine temperament, coupled with ability in the Field, the show ring, and in Obedience. Dual Ch. Gordon Hill Chantilly Lace CD, sibling to two all breed Best in Show winners, was herself a National Specialty BOS winner, and she produced two Dual Champion offspring among her six Champion produce. Since 1981, when Muriel Clement retired from breeding Gordon Setters, the Gordon Hill name and line has been carried on by Susan DeSilver.

GREYCOACH

Owned by Barbara Koch, Minnesota. Breeder and/or owner of Specialty winning Gordons.

GREENGLEN

Owned by Jim & Alyce Westphal, Minnesota. Known especially for its bitches: Greenglen bitches earned the Best of Opposite Sex award at three of the first six GSCA National Specialties. These bitches have also been top producers, and the foundation of other Gordon kennels in the US.

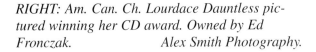

ABOVE: Greycoach Winteridge Willow: A young representative of the Greycoach kennel, owned by Barbara Koch.

RIGHT: Am. Can. Ch. Lourdace Dauntless pictured winning her CD award. Owned by Ed Fronczak.   Alex Smith Photography.

HALCYON
Owned by Steve & Laura Bedford, Connecticut. From the first litters bred in 1975 to the present, Halcyon has worked toward consistency, producing successful hunting dogs who fit the Breed Standard. Many have attained their Bench Championships, and several have also become Field Champions.

HEAVENLY
Owned by Loree Ragano, Illinois. A small kennel, Heavenly is best known for its multi-generation top producing sires, beginning with Am. Can. Ch. Rockaplenty's Hang 'Em High, sire of over forty American Bench Champions; continuing with his son, Ch. Rockaplenty's Ultimatum, also sire of over forty American Bench Champions, a Master Hunter, and a Dual Champion; and through to his son, Ch. Heavenly's Current Choice, sire of over ninety American Champions to date. Each of these sires has produced Specialty and Group winning offspring. This kennel also co-owned and campaigned the multiple Group placing and multi-Specialty winning bitch, Ch. Rockaplenty's Sooner Victory, in the early 1980s.

JP & S
Owned by Ellyn & Dave Jones & Maryann Leonard, Michigan. Established earlier as a Great Dane kennel. Gordons joined the strength in the late 1970s with the foundation sire, Am. Can. Ch. Lakeacres Thunderbolt, who proved to be a top producer. JP & S has produced

Dual Ch. Halcyon Guarantee Nothing, owned by Steve and Laura Bedford.

Chuck Tatham.

JP's Heavenly Hallmark Sastya.

many Bench Champions, including Specialty winners, and strives for a Gordon that will be a hunter, and a family companion that is beautiful to look at.

JONCYN
Owned by John & Cindy Smith, Michigan. Breeders and/or owners of many American and Canadian Champions, Specialty winners, and Obedience and Hunting titlists.

JOYOUS
Owned by Anita Lustenberger, New York This kennel has bred Gordons since 1952. Anita

has been active in publications for and about Gordon Setters and served for a number of years as the GSCA American Kennel Club delegate.

KA-DAN LANES
Owned by Dan & Karen Arterberry, Illinois. Established in 1973 with the goal of producing "bonny, balanced and birdy Gordons." Am. Can. Ch. Stilmeadows Jenny Leigh, passed these qualities to her daughter, Ch. Ka-Dan Lane's Carrie McDuff, and 'Carrie' in turn has passed them on to her offspring.

Ch. Ka-Dan Lane's Carrie McDuff, owned by Dan and Karen Arterberry.

KILERNAN
Owned by H.R. & Barb Manson, Wisconsin. This kennel believes the quality of future generations is dependent on the quality of their bitches, the most being Ch. Greenglen's Glad Rags and Ch. McErin Illustrator, CD. The Mansons are breeders and/or owners of multiple Specialty winning Gordons.

LOCUST GROVE
Owned by Sally Ann Walker, LVT, Michigan. This small kennel strives to produce Gordons capable of earning the GSCA "Beauty, Brains & Birdsense" honour. The foundation bitch, Am. Can. Ch. Heavenly's Current Bella Star WD, JH, Am/Can CD, WD, CCGCTT has earned titles in all three areas. Her offspring are competing for their own BBB awards.

L.T.K
Owned by Susan & Louis Oneppo, Rhode Island. Breeders of Specialty winning youngsters.

MACALDER
Owned by Tom and Deb Olson, South Dakota. This kennel dates back to 1964 and credits the early bloodlines to Marion Wilcox of the Afternod kennel. The founders of the kennel, Chuck and Bernie Stephenson, possessed an unwavering commitment to "breed type" that led to the development of a line breeding programme which now spans thirty years and is known for consistently producing classic Gordon Setter, type. The Stephensons' efforts were joined by Tom and Deb Olson in the 1970s as partners. Historically, the brood bitches and stud dogs of MacAlder kennel have had significant impact on Gordon Setter type in the

Am. Can. Ch. MacAlder Mr Chips: A Best in Show winner, and a prepotent stud dog for the MacAlder kennel. Owned by Tom and Deb Olson.

Carl Lindemaier.

United States and in Canada. Collectively, Am. and Can. Ch. MacAlder Mr. Chips; his son Am. and Can. Clansmen Colourgard; his son Am. and Can. Ch. MacAlder Clansmen Ian; and his son Ch. MacAlder Upland Hunter produced nearly two hundred American and Canadian Champion offspring. In addition to being prepotent stud dogs, these four also represent four consecutive generations of multiple GSCA Specialty Winners and Best In Show Gordon Setters. Currently, a son of Hunter, Ch. Brentwood's Magnum PI, is the top winning Gordon Setter in the US.

MACMARLEN
Owned by Kristin Majercik, Delaware. Established in the early 1970s with the emphasis on the all-round Gordon with title-holders on Bench, Field and Obedience competition.

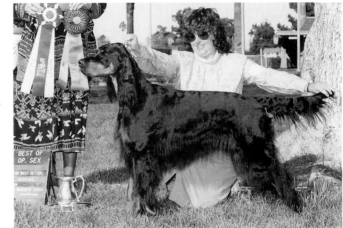

Ch. McErin's Like A Rock, bred and owned by Dean and Jane Matteson.

MACTYKE

Owned by Teresa V. Popham & Susan Randall, Michigan. Known for both Gordon Setters and Clumber Spaniels; Gordons were introduced in 1976. Breeders and/or owners of multiple Specialty winners, group winners and top producing sires and dams.

MCALLISTER

Owned by Ralph & Marie Jackson, Wisconsin. A small hobby kennel of relatively new origin, the Jacksons value a dog that is both a good hunting companion and a superb family friend.

MCERIN

Owned by Dean & Jane Matteson, California. Breeders of multiple Specialty winning Gordons. Owners of the multiple Best in Show winning Ch. Wylynd's Blue Thunder. Dean was the co-ordinator of the 1978-1988 *Gordon Setter Review* and wrote the chapter on "Gordons In The Ring" with his wife Jane. Jane is a contributing editor to *Gordon Quarterly* magazine, and she chaired the 1992 GSCA National Specialty.

McQ

Owned by Richard & Mary Quaco, Colorado. McQ produced the GSCA Brood Bitch of the Year 1982, GSCA Novice Obedience Dog 1983, multiple Specialty winners, the first US Gordon to earn the Tracking Dog Excellent title, as well as dogs who have earned their Junior Hunter titles. Richard is the current president of the Gordon Setter Club of America.

MOROCO

Owned by Mirtha Mortera, Puerto Rico. Perhaps the most well-known dog from this kennel was World Champion Moroco's Medicine Man, who earned Championships in the US, Puerto Rico, Venezuela, and Peru, as well as being named a South American, International and Bi-Peruvian Champion.

MOUNTAINVIEW

Owned by Shareen Brown, New York. Breeder of multiple Specialty-winning and Group-placing dogs. Shareen has worked in association with Laura Bedford of Halcyon Gordons for a number of years.

NICKEVEN

Owned by Fred Engler, Kansas. Producer of fine foot-hunting Gordon Setter pups.

RIVERMIST

Owned by Barry Goodman, Maryland. This kennel owned the 1980 Bench Gordon of the Year, Ch. Warlock's Windjammer. Responsible for many Specialty winners, and the all-breed Best in Show winning bitch, Ch. Rivermist Periwinkle. A number of Rivermist sires and dams are at, or near, top producer status.

ROCKAPLENTY

Owned by Elizabeth (Clark) Loveless, Virginia. Gordons have been bred at this kennel since the late 1960s, and it has produced many Champions, Specialty winners, Group winners and Best in Show dogs, as well as top producing sires and dams. Owner of Ch. Afternod Yank of Rockaplenty CD and Ch. Rockaplenty's Pit-A-Pat, who are still the breed's top producing sire and dam. Breeder of the Best in Show Ch. Rockaplenty's Run For the Roses and Ch. Rockaplenty's Real McCoy CD, among others. Rockaplenty Gordons are the foundation of a number of modern kennels in the US and Canada.

ROYALDELL

Owned by Virgina Kick, Michigan. Established in 1976, beginning with foundation, top producers Am. Can. Ch. Stilmeadows Darth Vader CD and Am. Can. Ch. Stilmeadows

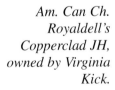

Am. Can Ch. Royaldell's Copperclad JH, owned by Virginia Kick.

Yesterday's Wish CD, and their daughter, Ch. Royaldell's Audacious WD, there have been four generations of Specialty-winning, Group-placing Royaldell Gordons. Many of these have also had Hunting and/or Obedience titles. Of note are Am. Can. Ch. Royaldell's Copperclad JH, with Field Trial placements, and his sister, Am. Can. Ch. Royaldell's Cover Girl CD, JH, WD, GSCA Beauty, Brains and Birdsense award winner.

SAMSON
Owned by Natalie Haberman, Massachusetts. A kennel name derived from the name of her first Gordon, 'Sam'. Mrs Haberman has produced Specialty winners and top producing Gordons.

SANDPIPER
Owned by Janice Beattie, Massachusetts. Breeder of Specialty, Group and Best in Show winning Gordons.

SASSENACH
Owned by Judith M. Brown. Judith's foundation Gordon was Am. Can. Ch. McErin California Dreamer CD ('Bailey'), who was from the Rockaplenty and MaCalder bloodlines. He was first bred to a Best in Show Am. Can. Ch. Fieldstone Buccaneer. From this union came Am. Can. Ch. Sassenach Pyjamarama. P.J. is a Canadian Speciality Breed Winner and has also proven herself to be a very valuable brood bitch. Although only producing small litters, quality and consistency came through. She was bred twice to the National Speciality Winner, Ch. Buteo's Colorado, and produced Group and Speciality winners, who are: Am. Can. Ch. Sassenach National Rendezvous (male), Am. Can. Ch. Sassenach Amas Gooseberry (female) and Am. Can. Ch. Sassenach a la Gooseberry.

Bailey's next litter, to Am. Can. Ch. MacAlder Clansman Ian, produced the Speciality

Am. Can. McErin California Dreamer with daughters Am. Can. Ch. Sassenach Pyjamarana and Ch. Sassenach H. Corbett.

winner and Group placer, Ch. Sassenach Tweed. Her brother, Ch. Sassenach Huey Lewis, proved to be an excellent Field dog.

SCIMITAR
Owned by Michael Osman & Janet Hawkins, Michigan. Mick judges AKC Hunting Tests, and he chaired the 1994 GSCA National Field Trial.

SHOJIN
Owned by Dee & Ron Vayda & Peggy Kelley, Michigan. Gordons have been bred at this kennel since late 1970s, and Shojin Gordons have earned titles in Conformation, Obedience and Field competition. Owners of Can. Mex. Am. Ch. MacAlder Best For Shojin, Specialty-winning, Group-placing, top producing sire.

SPRINGSET
Owned by Sue and Norm Sorby, California. This couple must be the most world famous Gordon Setter owners and breeders. Norman's book, *The Black and Tan Bombshell*, did much to spread their fame to all corners of the earth. Springset stock has been exported far

Norman Sorby pictured with littermates Springset Fabled Reality (left) and Springset Hot Sauce.

and wide; at least two Gordons came into the UK from this kennel. Norman Sorby was first introduced to Gordons in 1957 by the lady who was later to become his wife, Suzanne, the owner of Springset MacDuff.

This dog was Suzanne's first Gordon. It was some four years after they were married that the Sorbys seriously looked for another. They managed to obtain Springset Breeze from Alec Lawrence in 1962 and bred from this bitch to get their first litter, sired by Springset MacDuff. Since that time they have just kept going with Gordons.

While Norman was getting to know Breeze and her litter, he discovered that he was something of a natural where training was concerned. Subsequently, Norman has Field trained 3,217 dogs of all pointing breeds, and he has also done some Obedience training. Norm has been called the 'Father of the Gordon Setter', and the 'Guru of Gordon Setters', by virtue of his efforts to bring the Gordon back as a hunting and a Field Trial dog. To date, Springset is responsible for eighteen Bench Champions, three Dual Champions and forty-nine Field Champions. What a record!

STARBORN
Owned by Cathie & Ron Rzepka, Michigan. Originally associated with Scimitar Gordons, Mrs Rzepka has bred multiple Specialty winners and a Group-winning Gordon.

STILMEADOWS
Owned by Delores Gidday, Michigan. A breeder of Gordon Setters for over thirty years. This line was founded on Am. Can. Ch. Afternod Sybilla, dam to thirteen Champions. Her legacy goes on through her progeny. To date, this kennel has produced 167 Champions, with the aim of producing sound dogs, with fun-loving temperaments, excellent hips, true to the Breed Standard, and capable of a good day's work in the field.

SUN-YAK
Owned by Donald Sutherland, Washington. This kennel was established in 1948 by Mr Sutherland and his wife, Celeste. Sun-Yak Gordons have appeared in Gordon Setter Bench, Field and Obedience competition in North America for nearly fifty years.

SUNDANCE
Owned by Sally Puhalla, Illinois. This kennel is best-known for owning Ch. Berridale's Sundance Sarah, a top producing bitch with an impressive tally of sixteen Champion offspring. Multiple Specialty winners and Group placers have come from Sundance. Sally was the chair of the 1993 GSCA National Specialty.

SURESHOT
Owned by Bev & Bill Holoboff, Alberta, Canada. Gordons have been bred here since 1975, and the kennel has been active in Conformation, obedience and versatility competition. Owners of Am. Can. Ch. Clansmen Classic, top Gordon in Canada (dogs defeated) for 1993. Bev is the editor of the Gordon Setter Club of Canada newsletter and the Canadian correspondent for the Gordon Setter News.

Ch. Sureshot Clansman Camorra, owned by Bill and Bev Holoboff.

Mikron Photos.

TARTANA
Owned by Phil & Holly Wachuta, Wisconsin. Home of Dual Ch. Tartana Champagne Charlie CDX, WDR, MH, and breeder of the 1989 National Gordon Setter Open Shooting Dog (American Field) Champion Tartana Black Dodger. Tartana strives for dogs that can compete in breed, Obedience and Field competition, as well as providing loving family companions and hunting partners.

TEMMOKU
Owned by Julia Ouska & Lynn Fruchey, Colorado. Gordon Setters have been bred here since the mid-70s, with the emphasis on the sound, all-round Gordon.

TIMBARAY
Owned by Barbara Meining, DVM, Michigan. This is a new kennel, but the foundation bitch, Ch. Shojin's Spirit Of Timbaray UD, JH is already nearing top producer status. Her offspring have won Specialties and garnered High In Trial Obedience awards.

TOR DUBH
Owned by Ken & Pat Brate, New York. Gordons have been bred here since 1982, with the aim of producing the all-purpose Gordon who is a well-balanced stable companion for the home and Field. Breeder of Tor Dubh Pilmar MacMarlen UD, a top Obedience Gordon who has won the GSCA Obedience Annual Award for several consecutive years.

TOMAR
Owned by Anne Boyd, Virgina. Tomar Gordons have excelled on the Bench and in the Field.

Most notable is Field Ch. Tomar's Gone With the Wind JH, who sired the 1993 National Amateur Champion.

TOUCHSTONE
Owned by Camilla Anderson, Indiana. Gordons have been bred here since the early 1970s. Breeder of multiple Group and Specialty winning Gordons, many with Obedience titles.

TRI-SETT
Owned by Karen Gatchell, Connecticut. Breeder of many, many American Specialty winners and Group winners. The kennel is best-known for the all-breed Best in Show and National Specialty winning bitch, Ch. Tri-Sett Overboard Ahoy CD, and the Canadian Best in Show dog, Can. Ch. Tri-Sett Night Secret. Many Tri-Sett sires and dams have been GSCA top producers.

WILDWOOD
Owned by John, Virgina, Pamela & Jennifer Radonis, New York. Gordon Setters have been bred here since 1980. Breeder and/or owner of multiple Specialty-winning, Group-winning and all-breed Best in Show winning Gordons. Their bitch, Ch. Wildwood's Classic Design, was an all-breed Best in Show winner and a National Specialty winner in 1992 from the Veteran class. Her mother, Ch. Canterbury's Blue Velvet, was a Group winner and GSCA top producer. See also Bromwich.

WINTERIDGE
Owned by Bill & Genelle Stauder, Minnesota. This kennel has had several Specialty winning Gordons. Bill is the current Vice-President of the Gordon Setter Club of America.

WOODSMOKE
Owned by Cynthia Fitzgerald, Connecticut. Woodsmoke Gordons began in 1975 with 'Luke', a hunting dog, and has continued to try to maintain 'Saturday hunting, Sunday showing' Gordons. Cynthia says: "We show them for a hobby, hunt them for sport, and love them as family members." With limited breeding, the kennel has enjoyed considerable success, always maintaining a rule of 'quality above quantity'. Owner of Ch. Gordon Hill Alabama Slammer, Specialty and Group winner, and his Specialty and Group winning son, Ch. Woodsmoke's Classic Alibi. These sires have produced offspring with many Specialty wins, including several National Specialty winners, all-breed Best in Show winners, Obedience and Hunting-titled get.

WYTTSEND
Owned by Dianne Avery & Beni Levi, Michigan. This is a small hobby kennel, started in 1974, which is proud to have bred the Winners' Bitch at the first National Specialty in 1983, Ch. Wyttsend's Animation. Breeders and/or owners of a number of other Specialty winners, Hunting titlists, and Obedience titlists. Co-owners of Ch. Rockaplentys Ultimatum, a top producing sire, whose offspring have excelled in Conformation, Obedience and Field activities.

Chapter Thirteen

THE GORDON IN AUSTRALASIA

AUSTRALIA

Although Gordon setters have not been established for very many years in Australia, they have been fortunate enough to attract some caring and dedicated owners and breeders. The growth of the Gordons can be seen through these descriptions of some of the major kennels.

CLANSET

Meg MacCormick's small but successful kennel has, since it was first registered in 1982, bred a total of five litters, three of which have produced six Champions. The most notable dogs have been Champion Warchant Harmony and her sire, Champion Clanset Jass Duke.

Harmony, whose dam was Ch. Warchant Skye Lass, dominated the Specialty shows in Australia from 1987 to 1992. During this period twelve Specialty Championship shows were held, with Harmony winning Bitch Challenge and Best in Show on six occasions, and Bitch Challenge and Runner-up in Show on another three occasions. These wins were under both

Ch. Warchant Harmony, handled by her owner, Meg MacCormick.

English and American judges. She also won another three Championship Best in Shows, including one all breeds show, and has produced three litters for Clanset. Duke, sired by Ch. Glenlochay Fraser and whose dam was Ch. Warchant Ladybird, gained his title easily and had many good show wins, including an All Breeds Championship Best in Show.

The kennel is very aware of the need to breed sound dogs and has actively promoted hip X-raying and scoring. Most sires, and all the dams, of the Clanset litters have been scored and, so far, over a quarter of the dogs bred by the kennel have also been scored. As a result, more dogs from this kennel have been scored using the BVA scheme than from any other Gordon kennel outside the UK. The kennel is consistently gaining low hip scores – the average is 4.5.

To its Warchant foundation stock of the early eighties, which was a blend of Australian blood and that of the first American import, Am. Aust. NZ. Ch. Sutherland Hallmark, the kennel has recently introduced the blood of Am. Aust. Ch. Rockaplentys Quest for Roses, and has produced some very promising young stock.

LATCHMERE

Mick and Carol Nicol's Ch. Latchmere Navajo Joe, known as Rocky, had something special about him from the moment he was born – an air of arrogance saying 'look at me'. From the moment he stepped into the show ring, Rocky was winning Group awards. As he matured, he proved to be one of the biggest winning Gordons of all time and went on to rewrite the record books, winning at All Breeds, Gundog and Specialty Shows.

Rocky was from the first litter Latchmere bred. His sire was Am. Aust. Ch. Rockaplenty

Ch. Latchmere Navajo Joe (Am. Aust Ch. Rockaplenty's Quest for Roses – Ch. Triseter Black Miranda): A prolific winner for the Latchmere kennel.

Quest for Roses, imported from the USA, and his dam was Ch. Triseter Black Miranda. He himself went on to sire many Champions, including the current top winning Ch. Rokeena Black Appollo and Ch. Triseter Black Vader. His name appears in many of the current Gordon pedigrees. Sadly Rocky died of cancer at just seven years of age and is greatly missed by his human family; his memory lives on in his offspring.
Some of his most notable wins include:
1986 Best in Show Gordon Setter Club of NSW Specialty
1987 Best in Show Expo International Greensborough District Kennel Club All Breeds
1987 Best in Show Expo International Kilmore Kennel Club All Breeds
1987 Best in Show Gordon Setter Club of NSW Specialty
1988 Best in Show Gordon Setter Club of Victoria Specialty
1989 Best in Show Setter Club of South Australia Specialty
1987 1988 1989 1990 Gordon Setter Club of Victoria Dog of the Year.

The two Expo International Shows were special wins, as no other breed of dog has managed to win two All Breed shows in one weekend under International judges.

Carol and Mick also bred, and own, two other notable champions. Ch. Latchmere High Flyer, born April 26th 1989 and known as Flyer, resulted from the second Latchmere litter, sired by Ch. Rokeena Black Appollo, a Rocky son, out of Ch. Latchmere High Sierra, Rocky's sister. Flyer also was an early winner in the ring and has, in the past year, established his reputation by winning Best in Show and Best inGroup awards. Flyer's loving nature has endeared him to many and, with his mum and sister, he is happiest chasing tennis balls in the paddocks. Flyer has been used at stud, with his progeny currently having success in the show ring.
Some of his notable wins include:
1992 Dog Challenge & Runner-up to Best in Show Gordon Setter Club of Victoria Specialty
1992 Winner Sires Progeny Gordon Setter Club of Victoria
1993 Best in Group Australia Day International Show
1993 Best in Show A.C.T. Gundog Society Show
1993 Best in Show Gordon Setter Club of Victoria Specialty
1993 Winner Sires Progeny Gordon Setter Club of Victoria Specialty Show.

Ch. Latchmere Cast a Spell, from the same litter, and known as Frisco, has also had success in the show ring at an early age, often vying with her brother, Flyer, for BoB. Frisco's most notable win was Gordon Setter Club of Victoria Bitch of the Year 1992. She is happiest roving the paddocks and has the most endearing nature. Mick is currently campaigning Flyer's son.

Mick also co-owns, with Viv McLaughlin who bred him, a dog called Charlie. Korac Kingsford Smith, born January 19th 1992, is the most loving character and is doing well in the ring.
His wins include:
1993 Runner up to BoB Adelaide Royal
1993 Runner up to BoB Setter Club of NSW
1993 Junior in Show Gordon Setter Club of Victoria.

TRISETER

Esther Joseph first came into Gordons some twenty-three years ago. At that time she already
owned and showed Irish and English Setters, which she campaigned through to their titles.
She started with a male Gordon, Warchant Amber Rim, and then added a bitch puppy, Carli
– Ch. Fieldpride Blue Carli, to give her her full name. Carli was sired by Ch. Ledearle Rebel
Scot, from Fieldpride Contessa, whelped in 1971. Carli's breeder only had three litters
between 1967 and 1976.

Esther registered her prefix, Triseter (the three setters), as she planned to breed the three
breeds of setter – English, Irish and Gordon. As it has turned out, she has only bred English
and Gordons and, in the latter years, Gordons only.

Carli's first litter was to Ch. Warchant Drummer Boy, a top winning NSW dog at that time.
There were very few Gordons being shown in Victoria. Esther was determined to change this
and promote the breed. Three pups from her first litter went through to their titles, with a very
limited amount of Group winning.

The arrival of the American import, Am. Aust. & NZ Ch. Sutherland Hallmark, was very
exciting for Australian Gordons. Guy was his name at home. He was imported by the late Mr
G. Lack. Carli was mated to Guy and put his first litter on the ground in March 1976. This
litter was a great success, with six of the eight whelps going through to their titles. Four of
these dogs were campaigned regularly, and were foundation stock for new Gordon kennels,
two of which are still around today. Esther kept two bitches and a dog. She lost the dog in a
car accident, but the two bitches and two other male littermates did a lot of winning in the
breed and started to make an impact at Group level. Ch. Triseter Black Annwen (Ella) by
Guy out of Carli, was Gordon Setter Clubs Bitch of 1980 and 1981. She opened the door on
the show scene for her daughter, Ch. Triseter Black Nara, sired by Ch. Doonbrae Glen Scotia.
Black Nara was Bitch of the year in 1985, 1986 and 1987, also winning runner-up in Group
3 at Sydney Royal show in 1987, with many other in Group and Show awards.

A Gordon, called Neidpath McLeish, was imported from the UK by Mr G. Fraser. There
was only limited use of this dog, but his progeny include Aust. & NZ Ch. Triseter Black
Vader, and Am. & Aust. Ch. Rockaplenty Quest for Roses, known as Paul. Paul was another
dog that did not have enough bitches visiting, due to the petty jealousies which do sometimes
get in the way of intelligent breeding in the canine world. It was only at the end of his stud
life that people realised his worth. He had been imported by Mr R. Wallis and was put to a
number of Triseter Bitches, one of them being Ch. Triseter Black Miranda who produced Ch.
Latchmere Navajo Joe, the famous Rocky. He was put over Ch. Kgrae Kirrie Krista, whose
breeding is Ch. Glade Famos Amos out of Triseter Black Kirsty, to produce Aust. & NZ Ch.
Triseter Black Vader.

Rocky and his son Vader have done a lot for the breed in the show ring. Rocky is now
deceased but, before his premature death, his last mating was a repeat of the mating that
produced Vader. The result, Triseter Ebonie Colby, is now being shown, at two and a half
years of age. Esther hopes that he will come on. Vader is still being shown at seven years,
with a grand record behind him, having won eleven Best in Show awards, eight runner-up in
Shows, twenty-five Best in Group 3 and fifteen runner-up in Group 3. Three-quarters of his
Best in Show wins were at All Breed Championship Shows. Also Vader has won Best in

Ch. Latchmere Cast a Spell (Ch. Rokeena Black Appollo – Ch. Latchmere High Sierra).

Ch. Triseter Black Annwen: Bitch of the Year in 1980.

Group, Canberra Royal Show, and Best in Group, Adelaide Royal Show; and his latest, and most prestigous win, was runner-up Group 3, at Melbourne Royal Show, 1993.

Three-year-old Ch. Triseter Ebonie Belle (Latchmere High Flyer out of Triseter Black Xtasy) is a Gordon Setter Club of Victoria Bitch of the Year 1993 and an In Group and In Show winner. She also has a litter on the ground, sired by Swanley Strathfeshie, imported from the UK.

Two young dogs, litter brother and sister, Ch. Triseter Ebonie Dude and Ch. Triseter Ebonie Dallas, by Rokeena Black Thor out of Triseter Black Witch, have both been shown extensively over an eighteen month period, with both gaining their titles and having very good wins at Open Show level. Dude has two Best in Shows, four Best in Groups and Dallas has Two Best in Shows and six Best in Groups and many classes in Group and Show award at Championship Shows level. Dude was mated to Krista (Vader's mother) and produced two pups alive, Innika and Inxs. Innika stayed with Esther and is showing a lot of promise, but, as Esther says, only time will tell.

In 1978 Esther, together with Robyn Wallis, imported a pup from Barbara Summers. His name was Rhovanion Royal Emissary (Burnbreck Herb of Grace out of Salters Penny Royal of Rhovanion). Unfortunately Royal met with an accident, which resulted in his death, and he had only been used on a few bitches. Esther only breeds one or two litters per year and always to get something for herself.

Gordon Setters are now very competitive and are a real threat to all other breeds in the Gundog Group in Australia, especially in Victoria, where Esther feels that the breed is strongest. Australian winning Gordons could compete anywhere in the world and do very well. They have sound bodies under a profuse coat. Esther considers that the coat is necessary to be able to win at Group and Show level, but the dog must have type and soundness first. Esther is of the opinion that one should be able to pick a puppy of quality because it will stand out, and, if it grows coat, then it is a bonus.

WARCHANT

Dawn Ferguson always assumes that she inherited her love of animals. She was guarded by a cattle dog as a baby and, while growing up, was assisted by experience with Kelpies, Pugs, Irish Terriers, Cattle dogs and Stompy Tails, German Shepherds and Irish Setters. After she was married, she bred Cocker Spaniels and Irish Setters, until raising a young family interrupted dog activities. In 1960 Dawn and family became involved with Dobermans and, at this time, registered the Warchant affix. Dawn had intended to go back to Cockers until she saw her friend Julie Dickinson, who had an imported Gordon Setter bitch, with her litter. Choosing a bitch puppy was the start of a long obsession with Gordon Setters.

Two years later Dawn was still searching for a suitable sire, looking anywhere in Australia and finally finding a worthy dog in Victoria. This was Lederle Majestic Scott, who was owned by Mr Mimo Perna, used for hunting and only shown sparingly. The first litter by him produced fourteen puppies – thirteen survived. Out of this litter, seven were sold to show homes, became Champions and were the foundation of other kennels. The other six were also worthy specimens and could have won in the show ring. Champions from this first litter were: Warchant Majestic Scott, Warchant Drummer Boy, Warchant Black Earl, Warchant Kirribilli Lad, Warchant Will O'The Wisp, Warchant Whimsical and Warchant Piper – the last two being also CD achievers.

Ch. Warchant Drummer was the first Gordon to win Best in Show (All Breeds) and was the foundation of the Gooree kennel, Ch. Warchant Piper CD started the Merrowlea kennel, Ch. Warchant Black Earl started the Bernadel lines and Ch. Warchant Whimsical CD became the foundation bitch for the Doonbrae, while Ch. Warchant Will O'The Wisp became the foundation of the Daneson kennel. Warchant Majestic Lass was never shown but bred a litter for the Huntsman kennel.

Ch. Warchant Scots
Whimbre
(Piperhill Eilan Angus
– Piperhill Lorna Dee).

Ch. Warchant Majestic Scott was the sire of Ch. Doonbrae Glen Scotia, who was a prolific winner, from a mating to his niece from Whimsical Scott. Scott was a dog with an outgoing nature, temperamentally sound and with good bone and colour. His semen was stored and frozen when the procedure first became available and is still in storage. Warchant also acquired two hunting bitches from Victoria. Ch. Wanalta Sue proved an excellent mother and show bitch. Both she and Wanalta Lady Marcel were a delight to own and to live with. They kept in good health and grew old gracefully, both dying at the age of fourteen.

Dawn imported frozen semen from a British dog in New Zealand, with no success. Later she imported a bitch of British breeding, but this did not seem to blend in, so she did not continue with this line. When the American dog, Am. Aust. & NZ Ch. Sutherland Hallmark QC arrived, he was a welcome outcross. Indeed, most bitches in Australia were put to him. In 1985 Dawn ordered a dog from the MacAlder kennels in the USA, and imported Am. Aust. Ch. MacAlder Innes of Warchant CD. He was not what Dawn had originally wanted but, nevertheless, he was a quality dog and a proven sire in the top five in the USA. Sadly he died from cancer at only seven years of age, but his semen is also in storage.

Some of the successful Warchants have been sired by Ch. Warchant Dandy UD. He was owned by John Carter of Queensland. Ch. Warchant Heather was the productive foundation bitch for the Piperhill kennel in South Australia with her brother Replica, also a Champion. Both of these Gordons were sired by W. Majestic Scott from his sister, Majestic Lass. There were five title holders in the litter.

In one litter Dawn only had two pups and kept them both, Ch. Little Wonder and Ch. Little Viking. Little Wonder was Best Bitch and runner-up Best in Show at the Victorian first Gordon Setter Club Show. She had many successes and produced two great litters by Sutherland Hallmark QC. Seven of these became Champions. Ch. Warchant Coronet, from the second litter, went to Piperhill and was the dam of Ch. Piperhill Flash Gordon, whose sire was Ch. Doonbrae Glen Scotia. Flash was one of Dawn's most noted Gordons and she went back to him in another generation.

Ch. Warchant Crest was also a gem at home, twice Best in Show at the Setter Club, and, with multiple group wins, was then mated back to her father, Hallmark, or Guy as he was known at home. Ch. Warchant Cabriole UD ET was the first Gordon to have an Endurance title. Her sister Fleur De Lys, when put to Dawn's Am. Aust. Ch. MacAlder Innes of Warchant CD, another American import, produced Brodruggan Le Magician, the only Field Trial Champion Gordon in Australia. The brother went to establish the Clanset kennel with Ch. Warchant Lady Bird.

Ch. Warchant Scots Wimbre, also a multiple Best in Show winner with his sister Ch. Warchant Forest Fairy, went to start the Tarem Kennels. Ch. Warchant Lorne and Sye Lass went to begin the Troylorne Kennel. Another winner, Ch. Warchant Harmony, is very well known. She had been sold, for showing, to people in the country who did not get around to it, and was given back when she produced an unplanned litter. Since that time she has soared to unexpected heights with her many Best in Show awards for Clansett.

Dawn sent a nice bitch, by her MacAlder dog out of Crest, to New Zealand. Carolina Lee is a NZ and Aust. Champion and she has established a successful line for the Cameronian Kennels there. Warchant Heart to Heart CDX is another Obedience success for Ann Fitzgerald, as is her Warchant Ring Macduff CD. Ann owned the very first Gordon to get its UD title in Australia years ago – Warchant Tapestry UD.

More recently, having been denied access to one of her recent lines, Dawn has gone to include blood from Rokeena, with American Rockaplenty in the pedigree and, even more recently, to the Triseter kennel for access to some of the older generations of Glade included. She finds it exciting now to have more good sires to form a gene pool than she has ever had before and, with access to overseas sires as well, many possibilities are opened up.

NEW ZEALAND

BLACK WATCH

This successful kennel is owned by Bruce and Sylvia Robson. Bruce blames his sister Isabel for his involvement with Gordons. After a series of rented properties in the city, Bruce decided that if they moved into the country they could at last own a dog. In August of 1972 they moved out of the city to a place in the country and began the search for a dog. Bruce and Sylvia had always fancied an Irish Setter, but were dissuaded by Bruce's sister who said: "If you get one of those stupid things I shall disown you."

In October of that year she phoned again and said: "What you want is a Gordon Setter. There is a litter up here with the two best dogs still available. You can have your pick. You can choose the names Angus and Scott. I am paying half because I am getting married in February and we are coming to live with you and graze a horse on your property. You can collect your puppy at my wedding." Bruce and Sylvia's reponse was – "What is a Gordon Setter?" However, when they realised that this was obviously inevitable, they went to see the pups after the wedding, took one look, and fell in love with Gordon Setters for life.

They showed Angus and he gained his title but sadly, with no competition in the breed. He won Best of Breed at the National Dog Show out of a grand total of two Gordons. This was the first time he had ever had to compete with another Gordon Setter! In November 1973 Bruce and Sylvia met a visitor from Britain, Dr John Pitts, who had a Gordon bred by Tony Fanning in Yorkshire. Through John they arranged to purchase a pair from the Cuprea kennels. Tony Fanning was, at this time, planning to emigrate to Canada, and Tony offered a bitch bred by Mrs Haigh, Black Swan of Cuprea, and a dog out of a litter sired by Carelanrig Adonis out of Cuprea Black Queen – a bitch he was taking to Canada with him. The bitch subsequently gained her title and the dog was Cuprea Macduff.

All arrangements were made and the Fannings duly moved to Canada in June 1974, just before the Gordons for Bruce and Sylvia left for New Zealand. However, there was a mix-up with the export requirements and it was not until after the flight arrived in New Zealand that the Robsons realised that the puppies were not on the plane. Yvonne Horrocks in the UK kindly intervened and discovered that the pups could not leave Britain as their rabies shots were not done in time as the Ministry of Agriculture demanded a time lapse of thirty days after the shot before the animal may leave the country. Eventually all was resolved and they did actually arrive in September.

The long stay in kennels before leaving for New Zealand had sadly led to Macduff becoming rather shy with strangers and to a subsequent dislike of the show ring. Needless to say, both went on to gain their titles, whence they were retired to begin the breeding programme for Bruce and Sylvia, and were responsible for many successful Gordons.

A list of winners that these two were responsible for is enclosed later. It looks quite an epic performance when one sees the number of winners. The biggest winning dogs have all come from a mixture of English bloodlines with the American import, Sutherland Hallmark. This dog was imported into Australia by Graeme Lack. From a litter by him out of Black Swan of Cuprea, Black Watch Arran was kept: he won Reserve Best in Show awards twice as well as several Best of Group awards.

NZ Ch. Black Swan of Cuprea (Imp. UK), and (facing) Aust. Ch. Glengordan Lord Angus.

When Black Watch Battlemaid was mated to him the Robsons admit to this probably being the best litter they ever bred. Four of them were shown and all achieved their titles. From this litter came Black Watch Loch Rannoch, who was New Zealand's first Best in Show All Breeds winning Gordon. He was owned by Raewyn Anderson, who was at that time Raewyn Webb of Wanganui. The Robsons kept B.W. Loch Katrine, who won several Gundog Groups and also won Reserve Best in Show All Breeds. Raewyn Anderson showed and still has a son of Loch Rannoch – Ch. Webly Always Bryden who has twice won Best in Show All Breeds.

A half-sister to half-brother mating between Arran and Loch Katrine resulted in another top-class litter. Four from this litter also gained their titles and one of these was Ch. Black Watch Coral: known as 'Brenna', she became the foundation bitch for Deborah Addenbrooke of the Et Settera kennel. Later the Robsons bred many Group winning Gordons, but the best was Ch. Black Watch Bentley who was a house dog and pet. Bentley won Reserve Best of Group at an All Breeds Championship Show at the age of six years. He also won several Group awards as a younger dog.

ET SETTERA

Deborah Addenbrooke's first initiation into Gordon Setters was in November 1982 when she purchased a foundation bitch from the Black Watch kennel of the Robsons. This bitch was Ch. Black Watch Coral and was affectionaly called 'Brenna Bugs'. It seems that from that moment on, life was never the same, and as Deborah says, this bitch gave her a cracker of a life. Brenna won seven Groups and two as a puppy. She took three Group awards in the Intermediate class, and she also won four Novice Field Trials and was awarded a third and a fourth place in Novice Obedience Tests.

Her first litter was the result of a mating to Black Watch Dragoon (NZ Ch. Cupra Macduff, import from the UK – Ch. Black Watch Battenmaid). One puppy was the end product and he was named Et Settera Bugsy Malone. Sadly, his show career came to an early end when an accident necessitated the amputation of a large section of his tail – however, not before he had won five Groups – (two as a puppy; one as a Junior) and several Field Trial placings. Ch. Black Watch Zephyr, a second acquisition of Deborah's, produced a litter – all of which went to working homes. One of these, namely Et Settera Capri-Britt, won several Novice Field Trial placings, then she moved on to a solid working home – total bliss for this bitch who had no other real interest.

Brenna had two more litters. In the second one all the Gordons worked for their owner, and from the third came a pup who was shown and gained her title, before going on to live with a family. The reason for the finish to her show career was an accident which left her handicapped with a problem to do with balance. 'Chess', as she was known at home, was the Pointer and Setter Club's Top Puppy in 1989.

Deborah was especially pleased with her last two litters, one sired by the top NZ winning Gordon – NZ Ch. Canockbrae Matouka Mac. These were all sold to working homes, although Et Settera Oban will be shown by Deborah. Deborah has also bred Malone to Ch. Black Watch Melba (QC) and she hopes that this litter will back up her show/working plans for future years.

Ch. Et Settera Bugsy Malone (left) and Ch. Et Settera Chess resting between retrieves from the water.

OTHER SUCCESSFUL BREEDERS

RAEWYN ANDERSON with Ch. Black Watch Loch Rannoch and his son Ch. Weblyn Always Bryden.

JILL HARDING won Field Trial Challenges with her home-bred dog Ch. Invergordon Black Duke. He gained his show title and was very close to getting his Field Trial Championship when he was tragically stolen, escaped, and was run over when he was almost home.

JIM COBURN of Rotbrua is competing successfully in Obedience with Gordons.

OLGA HENTHORN has won Best in Show All Breeds with her Australian imported dog Ch. Alderwood Ashen Fleet. She is currently winning Gundog group after Gundog group with his son, her home-bred Ch. Canockbrae Matouka Mac. I believe that his best win so far is Reserve Best in Show All Breeds.

MICHELLE CORLEY has won Best in Show All Breeds with her home-bred Ch. Banffshire Kilted Piper.

Chapter Fourteen

THE GORDON IN EUROPE

THE EUROPEAN BACKGROUND

France, Holland and Belgium, together with Norway, Poland and Sweden, did not fare any better than the UK during the years of World War II, that is from 1939 until 1946. Most of the pedigree dogs, if not confiscated by an advancing and invading army, were put down.

Freidal Van Dam, who came to Britain from Holland in 1946, had many stories to tell and one of them was that, as the invading army arrived, orders were given for all the residents in one of the villages to report to the local square and bring their dogs with them. As these were the very early days of the Occupation, everyone was very naive as they all turned up at the appointed time, with no conception of what would be the result by the end of the next few hours. The meeting was to enable the invaders to give instructions about such matters as curfews. Then the people were told to come forward, one at a time, with their dogs. Some German Shepherds and similar breeds were confiscated, but others, who were not of the guarding type, were shot in front of their owners; adults and children alike witnessed this mass slaughter.

Very few Gordons existed after the war, unless they were owned by members of the German army. This is why, when life had regained something resembling normality, many Gordons were exported from Britain to the Continent and formed the foundations for many breeders who are prominent with their success today. Tracing pedigrees back, it is amazing how often one comes across a British Dog.

Freidal's arrival in the UK, complete with two Gordon Setters, was something of a miracle. It seems that the dogs survived the war because she was able to hide them in a cellar when she needed to. Speygrounds was her prefix and it is in many pedigrees.

Exports have left the UK shores to find their way into Finland, Sweden, Norway, Holland, Switzerland, France and Germany. Some breeders are also buying stock from America.

FIELD TRIALLING

Due to this wartime devastation, many of the sports such as hunting and shooting disappeared altogether, as the wild game required for these kinds of events was no longer available. Some species were totally wiped out and those that did survive were very small in number, so any kind of dog work had to take on a different face if the communities were to start again. I attended a Field Trial in France, the actual location being Dunkirk. This had been organised by the French Gordon Setter Club, for members only. They met at the local cafe and we waited while the catalogues were sold and arm bands for the handlers distributed. I was quite concerned as to where we would find any game, as the location, I had been told, was quite near to the beaches. However, while we were waiting at the cafe for the day to begin, it seemed that a trailer full of pheasants had arrived and emptied its contents onto the nearest piece of land we were to use.

The number of birds was calculated in accordance with the entry, at a rate of two and a half birds per dog. These were shot when the dog was asked to flush and the dog was expected to retrieve them to hand and be judged accordingly. The judges carried the guns.

All the dogs were very keen, as they quickly become aware that there would always be game present, and this enhanced their keenness to hunt. We stopped for lunch and there was a count of how many birds had been shot and, with regard to the number of entrants for the afternoon, more birds were added while we ate at the cafe.

Each dog was allowed to run for fifteen minutes, after which the handler was asked to pick up his dog. The winner was the dog who had accounted for the greatest number of birds in that time. It did not involve the large acreage needed in Britain, where only natural game is hunted.

PROFESSIONAL TRAINERS

In the UK, when the winter has been severe and many of the grouse and partridge have not survived in sufficient numbers to produce many chicks, running in a trial can be very disappointing, as there are no game to be found. The grouse moors are precious and owned by either wealthy landowners or by syndicates who organise and run them for sport, which starts on August 12th. There is so much money to be made by selling shooting rights, that those who trial are often not allowed on these grounds because they might disturb the birds which may be there. Obtaining suitable land is a jealously guarded art by those who manage to persuade a friendly gamekeeper to let them on. The result of this is that it is almost impossible to find people in the UK who train Setters and Pointers for a living. Most of those who compete are doing so with their own dogs and will not take anything in to train, partly because it would be so expensive and partly because they only have the use of sufficient ground to train their own dogs.

This is not so on the Continent, where there are many trainers who will take dogs and train for a living. Most of these are to be found in France and a particular one, whom I have seen work, is Christian Charron. He trains for the Karrers in Switzerland, though he works with many other Setters as well. I have to admire this man. To watch him at work – he is so quiet; and it is obvious, after just a few minutes, how much the dogs adore him. He seems to know what they are thinking and they appear to reciprocate.

PRIZE-GIVING

As a visitor at the Dunkirk field trials, I was allowed to walk near the judges and observe the dogs working quite close to me. At the end of the day the entire party returned to the same cafe and, to my surprise, there was a room prepared with a raised dais and neat rows of chairs. It seemed that this was prize-giving time. The Lord Mayor honoured us all with his company and had a brass band to announce his arrival. The pomp and ceremony was wonderful to witness. All the competitors and their families, together with all the Gordons, were present to witness the presentations to the winners. I smiled quietly as my thoughts went back to the last field trial I had attended in Britain. No glorious winning ceremonies there, just a few cars on a quiet roadside, and only the brave handlers who had persisted and not been put off by the miserable rain, stayed to applaud those lucky enough to receive an award!

INFLUENTIAL EUROPEAN KENNELS

HOLLAND

KINGS CASTLE
Andre and Lily Konoings started with two Gordon males. These were Jason vom Forsthaus Hattlich and Robinson van Huize Comtessa. Their sire was an import from England, Carorae the Cavalier. Jason's mother was of German breeding and Robinson's mother was an English bitch named Dulnan Countess. Robin was born in 1978 and Jason in 1980. They are now both Dutch Champions and have won many titles in Europe.

Andre and Lily also owned Chap William Box van Huize Comtessa. He was a son of Jason's litter brother, Jupp vom Forsthaus Hattlich, and the German Champion, Timadon Dee.

William was awarded Best of Breed when he was only seventeen months old, at the Dutch Gordon Setter Club's show (NGSC), and he was also a Luxemburg Show Champion. William suffered badly when he was in a car, with Andre and Lily, which was involved in an accident. His injuries were such that, although he made a good recovery, his movement was never as good as before and his show career came to an abrupt end.

In 1985 Jason was used at stud and Lily kept the pick of that litter. This was named Red Castles Charming Cleardance (Dancy); her mother was Cathy vande Ratanja and she was bred in Belgium. One year later, from another bitch that Jason had mated, came a puppy called First Lady of Happiness van los Perros (Lady); her mother was Daisy van los Perros and she was Dutch bred.

At the time of Dancy's arrival, Andre and Lily imported a puppy from England. This was from a litter sired by Sh.Ch. Lourdace Spectrum of Cranchester out of Sunstone Shady Lady of Triphen. This pup was named Triphen Magic Moments (Maggy). She was never bred from but, instead, had a very successful show career, winning many tickets, and is a Dutch Show Champion. In 1988 she was Best Bitch at the NGSC Show and, at the Bundessieger in 1988, Maggy, together with Jason, took the award for Best Bitch and Best Dog.

The first litter that Lily and Andre bred was from Dancy. They used a dog from Switzerland, Int. Ch. Blackberry Hawthorn, whose grandparents are Swanley Strathtay and Slaters Ilex, both of English breeding. From this litter, known as the 'Admiration' litter, came three Dutch Champions: they are Jumbo Admiration, Dusty Admiration and Sanna Admiration. Jumbo also became a German Show Champion and Europe Sieger. Dusty won

*Netherlands Ch.
Dusty Admiration
from Kings Castle.*

Ch. Danceur des Pierres du Jour: This German-based Gordon setter is of French breeding, and has excelled as a working dog and in the show ring.

Int. Ch. O'Gilli Bluebell (Cubus Ebony – Lourdace Mocking Bird).

at the Winners Show at Amsterdam and took the title of Winner 1991. Sanna won this same title in 1989, 1990, and 1992. Jumbo and Sanna were also Top Dog and Top Bitch at the Club Show of the NGSC in 1989, with Sanna repeating this performance in 1993.

The second litter bred was sired by Jumbo and came from Lady. This litter was the 'Beloved' litter. It produced three siblings who became champions: Beloved Treasure, Beloved Shelley and Beloved Sarah. At the Bundessieger Show of 1992 where I was the judge, I made Treasure Best of Breed. Shelley, at the Jubilee Show of the NGSC, judged by Sue Woodland (UK), was Best Bitch, and one year later Sarah was BoB at the same show and Shelley's son, Invergordons Pearly Faun, was Best Dog.

In 1993 Easy Dreamgirl, from Kings Castle, won the title of Dutch Show Champion. Her mother is a litter sister to Sanna, Girly Admiration. Dreamgirl's sire is Jason. Dreamgirl competed at Dortmund, Germany, and was World Junior Champion 1991. Her brother, Easy Listening, has to get two more tickets to gain his title, but 1993 saw Easy Dreamgirl and Easy Listening as Best Dog and Best Bitch.

Just a few weeks before Chap William Boss died, his last litter was born. He had been mated to Girly Admiration. From this litter a bitch was kept and named Happy Dark Angel from Kings Castle. She soon became Best Junior and Best Bitch at the Club Show 1991, judge Sue Woodland, and she won the Junior title in Amsterdam 1992. She stood Reserve at the Club Show of the NGSC 1993. Since 1985, when the Kings Castle Gordons made their debut, this kennel has won the Breeders Cup, presented by the Dutch Gordon Setter Club in 1988. This is due to the many Champions they have bred in that short time.

SWITZERLAND

O'GILLI

Erwin and Heidi Karrer started their kennel in 1984, purchasing a foundation bitch from my Lourdace kennel. She was Lourdace Magnolia who after being sent to France for field trial

Blackberry Jass Duke: A Swiss-based Gordon Setter on point during a Field Trial.

training, was tragically killed in a road accident. However, Erwin returned to the UK and made a further purchase, Lourdace Mocking Bird. She was bred the same way as Magnolia but was from a later litter. Mocking Bird became their foundation bitch.

She was mated to Cubus Ebony, who had some ancient ancestry going back to UK stock but was otherwise of German blood. As hip dysplasia is a high consideration in Switzerland, it is interesting to note that this male was X-rayed clear. The one disadvantage was that he was very black in his colouring and lacked a really good rich tan. However, from this mating came two International Champions: one O'Gilli Bluebell, who qualified in the field before managing to beat her sister, O'Gilli Breeze, in a show event. Breeze reached great heights, being made World Champion in 1989.

Further purchases were made from the UK. One, a dog named Lourdace Bullion, was to achieve International Titles including World Champion. He also proved to be a very useful stud dog and was used by breeders from other countries as well as Switzerland. Bullion met a very untimely end when only six years of age and was put down to save further suffering from cancer. Erwin came again to the UK and purchased two more Gordons, a dog and a bitch, who were the litter mates Lourdace Bronco and Black Rose. Black Rose, the bitch, was bought on behalf of Werner Fink (Switzerland) and went on, in the show ring, to gain her International Title, as did the dog. One Gordon bred by the Karrers who is outstanding, is O'Gilli Ebony. He won his class at the breed club show, being marked 'Excellent' and was then trained to become an Avalanche Rescue Dog and a Search & Rescue Dog (used to search large wooded areas for lost persons) and has proved to be invaluable.

Sadly, in Switzerland, which is a very small country, there are few facilities for training a

Blackberry Jass Duke retrieving a pheasant.

O'Gilli Black Joggers Arron and O'Gilli Glenrose

dog for field work. Those who manage to do so have to live in the right location and have time to spare for it. Erwin Karrer sends his setters to France where the expert Frenchman I have mentioned, Christian Charron, takes them for periods of three months at a time to train for the field. The Karrers travel to France to learn too, and the dogs stay there for three months. The progress this kennel has made is seen in the following list of dogs from the Karrer breeding. Since 1984, when the kennel started, eleven litters have been bred. The breed's founders were Lourdace Mocking Bird and Lourdace Bullion. Subsequently, a three-generation female pedigree has produced very successful typical Gordon Setters.

Ruth Weis breeds Gordon Setters in Switzerland using her Blackberry prefix. Her stock has mixtures of British blood, and she has been to the UK on several occasions in order to buy in new stock. When I judged in Switzerland, I gave top award of the day to Int. Ch. Blackberry Hawthorn.